BASEBALL
LIFE MATTERS

BASEBALL LIFE MATTERS

AND

"The Team of the Ages"

A Celebration of Baseball,
a Championship Team,
and Life Connections

RICHARD GOODWIN, SR.

Contents

FOREWORD

The American Legion Baseball Program

The American Legion was chartered in the United States in 1919 and continues operations in all 50 states. Honorably discharged military veterans and military active duty, who served during wartime can become members of the American Legion. This book's author is a proud member of the American Legion. According to multiple sources, including *The American Legion Magazine*, currently there are approximately 1.8 million members. The National United States American Legion Baseball program was established in 1925, and the first national championship was played in 1926. The legion baseball program was designed to help promote sportsmanship, citizenship, good health, and equality. It was intended to provide an opportunity for youth to play baseball competitively at a high level and to help prepare young men for service to the United States, their families, and communities. Since its inception, it is estimated that more than 10 million youths have played American Legion Baseball. Also, a majority of all Major League baseball players and college baseball players have played American Legion Baseball. In short, American Legion Baseball has successfully provided a meaningful and lasting sports program, which has fostered the growth and development of our nation's youth for close to 100 years. The 1967 Ely Fagan team—players, coach, and manager—exemplify these core values.

COOPERSTOWN

When most people hear the word, "Cooperstown," they think of the Baseball Hall of Fame, and yes, it has been and still is, the home of the National Baseball Hall of Fame and Museum. There, museum visitors and baseball enthusiasts walk down hallowed halls, and comb through numerous player plaques, statistics, statues, pictures, and other baseball artifacts. The history of the game of baseball is well represented there, and the game itself, and the game's greatest players and their baseball accomplishments and records, are forever recognized and preserved.

Cooperstown village lies beautifully and peacefully at the southern end of Otsego Lake, in the central New York State region. In addition to housing the Baseball Hall of Fame, there's the historic Doubleday Field, named in honor of Abner Doubleday who, legend has it, had a hand in formulating the game of baseball. A section of the Erie Canal isn't far away, and Cooperstown also offers the Fenimore Art Museum, the Farmer's Museum, and the historic Otesaga Resort Hotel with its picturesque Leatherstocking Golf Course.

William Cooper founded the village—hence the name "Cooperstown"—and his son, famous writer James Fenimore Cooper, grew up there. James Fenimore Cooper may be best known for his writing of the Leatherstocking Tales, including *The Last of the Mohicans*. He saw Lake Otsego as his "Glimmerglass Lake," a name most befitting. Cooperstown is, for a variety of reasons, a place worth visiting.

But there's no denying, the game of baseball and Doubleday Field are permanently and forever woven into the fabric of Cooperstown, New York. From around 1940, through recent times, numerous Major League and Minor League exhibition games and "old timers" games, have been played on Doubleday Field. Some of the game's greatest teams and players have set foot onto, and played at, Doubleday Field. And for many years, Doubleday Field was also the site of the New York State American Legion Baseball Championship game. Now, the double-elimination state championship tournament is usually held in Utica, New York, over a period of a week or so. But for many, many years prior, only 2 teams met on Doubleday Field, on one day, and one game—and one game only—decided the New York State American Legion Baseball Championship.

Many professional baseball players and coaches across the

United States have played American Legion Baseball prior to entering the pro ranks. Lawrence "Yogi" Berra, Ted Williams, Tom Seaver, George "Sparky" Anderson, Johnny Bench, Richie Ashburn, Barry Bonds, Reggie Jackson, Frank Robinson, Brooks Robinson, Harmon Killebrew, Earl Weaver, Roger Clemens, Ron Guidry, Pee Wee Reese, Ralph Kiner, Chipper Jones, Carl Yastrzemski, Justin Verlander, Greg Maddux, Albert Pujols, Roy Campanella, Dusty Baker, and Bobby Cox are some of the famous, former American Legion Baseball players. Yes, since its inception in 1925, American Legion Baseball has provided youths with a history-rich, amateur league mechanism to play competitive baseball, and to learn and practice good sportsmanship and citizenship. And over those many years, millions of youths have played American Legion Baseball, with some then going on to play college baseball, and as mentioned previously, others moving on to the professional ranks.

Many legion players and teams have won local competitions, few have won state championships, and fewer still have emerged as legion baseball national champions. This book focuses on one remarkable upstate, New York State American Legion Baseball Championship Team, Ely Fagan Post from Henrietta, New York, and its players. The Ely Fagan American Legion Baseball team won the New York State Championship in 1967, and Ely Fagan is still the only Legion baseball team from the Rochester, New York, area to ever win the state championship. This is an account of the team's and players' journeys, baseball success, life success, and the life lessons the players learned.

We, the members of the Ely Fagan team, welcome those who read this baseball and life story, and especially those who are or were baseball players, to reflect on their own baseball and life journeys. We hope readers' baseball experiences and life insights are, or have been, as rich, meaningful, and memorable as ours.

INTRODUCTION

"In baseball, my theory is to strive for consistency, not to worry about the numbers. If you dwell on statistics you get shortsighted, if you aim for consistency, the numbers will be there at the end."
—Tom Seaver

During the summer of 2018, my former 1967 American Legion, New York State Championship Baseball Team—Ely Fagan Post, Rush-Henrietta, New York—was selected to be the Team of the Ages. Former team players—including yours truly—gathered in Rochester, New York, at Frontier Field baseball park (home of the International League baseball team, the Rochester Red Wings) to be honored and inducted into the prestigious Frontier Field Walk of Fame. Over 50 years had passed since we last played together, and for some of us, it was the first time in a very long time we had seen one another. We spent time reminiscing, catching up, sharing baseball and other sports stories, and really just sitting together, talking, reconnecting, and getting to know each other again after so many years of being apart.

Looking back, what I remember, and what I think set us apart from other Rochester-area baseball teams, was our unique team chemistry, and our willingness to be total team players. We pulled together every inning of every game we played, and had only one goal in mind—to win as a team through our collaborative efforts. Each of us celebrated success and the achievements of our fellow teammates. Each of us played unselfishly and believed only in supporting each other. Each of us played to win, and we never played to lose. We remained focused on each and every pitch and situation, between innings and while in the dugout or off the playing field. Yes, it was great fun to succeed. It was terrific to win. Rest assured, we played with intensity and desire, and when on the field, we played at a very high level of competency, rarely making physical errors or mental mistakes, and we met each situation, and challenge we faced, the best we could. And our terrific, supportive, and energetic coach, Harold Petersen, served as the essential sparkplug and catalyst for our individual and team success.

Maybe that's why we ultimately became the 2018 Team of the Ages. We were and still are, the only American Legion Baseball team from the Rochester area to EVER win the New York State American Legion Baseball Championship! And American Legion Baseball in New York State is big, prominent, and has been around for a very long time—over 95 years . . . lots of years, and lots of teams and players.

History, the many years of competition, and the baseball record books, have shown and validated our team's performance and unique success in 1967. I've continued to ask myself, "What was it about us and our team that set us apart from other teams?" "Why were we, and why are we still, the only Rochester-area Legion team to become New York State Champions?" After thinking about it, and allowing time for reflection, I reached out to fellow teammates to get their views and answers, and to provide their additional perspectives. Several players responded and have identified some of those reasons and answers, and together, we have discovered some of the essential ingredients for our baseball, and life, success.

These aren't just thoughts about baseball or our baseball experiences. More importantly, these are our thoughts about how those remarkable and special baseball experiences, culminating in being recognized as the Team of the Ages, helped shape our lives, helped shape us as athletes, and helped equip us with some of the essential mechanisms and tools needed to handle life's ups and downs, and to become happier, more resilient, and more effective citizens, leaders, teachers, parents, and coaches.

WHO WERE ELY AND FAGAN?

Our championship team played for the American Legion "Ely Fagan" Post located in Rush-Henrietta, New York. The Rush-Henrietta Legion Post #1151 was named after 2 men—Frank Ely and Arthur Fagan. Frank Ely was a sergeant in the United States Army and served during WWI. Arthur Fagan served during WWI in the capacity of 2nd lieutenant in the United States Army. Both Sergeant Ely and Lieutenant Fagan served our country with distinction in WWI. Sergeant Ely was from the town of Rush, and Lieutenant Fagan was from the town of West Henrietta.

THE 2018 WALK OF FAME INDUCTION

To quote from the 2018 Walk-Of-Fame official program: "Since 1977, a special section at the center of Frontier Field's Walk of Fame has been designated to recognize Rochester's sports legends. Each year, members of the community vote to induct individuals (fans, players, management, and media spanning Rochester's sports history) who have made a monumental impact on the community through their achievements in the Rochester-area sports scene. To commemorate these historic individuals, we add a brick with their name to the Walk of Fame during a select Rochester Red Wings game. This year we will be inducting 20 new members from 8 categories into the Frontier Field Walk of Fame."

The 2018 inductees were as follows:

Category	Inductees
Media	Wayne Fuller
Amateur Coaches	Chris Battaglia
	Nick DerCola
	Lysle "Spike" Garnish
	Duane McCoy
	Sally Wilkins
Amateur Sports	Tyler Relph
	Mindy Sawnor

Contributors/Administrator_____John Galipeau
Jill McCabe
Carm Urzetta

Professional Sports_____Eugene Goodlow
Chandler Jones
Andy Parrino

**Team of the Ages_____1967 Ely Fagan American Legion
NYS Champions**

Chairman's Choice_____1958 U of R Football Team

Olympians_____Paige Conners
Brian Gionta
Jonathon Lillis
Morgan Schild

We all arrived early to meet and then headed over to the special 11 a.m. VIP reception/barbeque. The Ely Fagan team members and guests in attendance greeted one another and spent time reconnecting and talking about their life experiences since their historic 1967 season. Then, the induction ceremony followed. Each of the inductees were announced and were welcomed and recognized by warm fan applause as they moved onto the field. Then there was the ceremonial brick placement in the Walk of Fame area to honor each of the inductees. After the brick placement ceremony, inductees relaxed in the stadium seats and enjoyed watching their hometown Rochester Red Wings play the Charlotte Knights!

Now, let's meet the team.

2018 Walk of Fame Induction, 8/12/2018, Frontier Field, Rochester, NY. The 1967 Ely Fagan Team of the Ages. Former players in attendance from left to right: Andy Haefner, Rene Piccarreto, Joe Haefner, Barb Petersen (scorekeeper), Chuck Glaza, Rich Goodwin (holding Walk of Fame commemorative brick), Bill Kreger, John Kokinda, Gary Junge, Al Goodwin (Bat Boy), Tom Pannoni (Bat Boy), Ralph Clapp, Al Pannoni.

THE PLAYERS AND POSITIONS

This is the Rush-Henrietta, New York, Ely Fagan Post, American Legion 1967 New York State Championship Baseball Team, coached by Harold Petersen.

Gary Junge—RH Pitcher

Gary was an outstanding, 3-sport and All-County athlete at Rush-Henrietta High School.

He was THE dominant pitcher in New York, and one of the finest high school pitchers in the USA. Gary played baseball at Clarkson University, Muni-League in Rochester, NY, for the Orleans Cardinals in the Cape Cod Baseball League, and signed with the Chicago Cubs organization after graduating from Clarkson. He played professionally for 6 years, rising to Triple-A level. Gary dedicated many years of his life to the Rush-Henrietta-area youth baseball and sports programs, and he has received numerous honors, including Hall of Fame honors, in recognition of his meaningful community contributions, and his outstanding performance in baseball. He was inducted into the Section V Hall of Fame in 2012, as part of its second class. Gary enjoyed many years in corporate business, serving in both management and executive level capacities.

Andy Haefner—RH Pitcher/Outfield

Andy was a leading, 3-sport and All-County athlete at Rush-Henrietta High School.

Andy was a hard-throwing righty, an outfielder with a rifle arm, and he has become one of Rochester's leading amateur golfers, winning numerous local and regional golf tournaments. Andy has been a successful Rochester-area businessman for many years.

Joe Baldassare—LH Pitcher/Outfield

Joe was a standout 3-sport and All-County athlete at East Rochester High School. Joe was a finesse pitcher with pinpoint control. He went on to play for Brockport State College.

John Kokinda—RH Pitcher

John was an outstanding, multisport, All-County athlete at East Rochester High School. He was a hard thrower, and he was a leading member of the World Champion 1966, East Rochester, New York, Senior League Baseball Team.

Joe Haefner—Outfield

Joe was an outstanding, 3-sport and All-County athlete at Rush-Henrietta High School.

Joe was a left-handed, power hitter, and he went on to play baseball at Auburn University where he set a number of hitting records, and where he earned Academic All-American honors. Joe went on to play championship, regional, and national level, slow-pitch softball. He has been a successful, Rochester-area business-man for many years.

Rene Piccarreto—Outfield

Rene was an outstanding, 3-sport and All-County athlete at Rush-Henrietta High School. Rene hit for high average and power, he played center field flawlessly, with speed, and a strong and accurate throwing arm, and he was lightning fast on the ba-ses. Rene starred in Muni-League play, and he went on to play Division I baseball for the University of Arizona and also at the University of Rochester, where he set a number of U of R school records. Subsequently, Rene became a United States Marine Corps officer, military leader, and fighter pilot, serving our country honorably for years. Rene has been a devoted educator for many years, serving as professor of business administration and management at Rochester Institute of Technology.

Al Pannoni—Shortstop/Pitcher

Al was one of Rochester's leading 3-sport and All-County athletes at Rush-Henrietta High School. Al was a quick, skilled, multitalented infielder and pitcher. Al was a star member of the 1961 New York State Championship Moose League Baseball team. Al went on to play baseball for Monroe Community College, and the Division I University of Buffalo. Al became an outstanding Rochester-area teacher and coach, and he has been honored with Hall of Fame recognitions for his teaching and coaching excellence.

Bobby Porta—Second Base

Bob was a steady and reliable infielder, and a dependable hitter. He was a multisport, leading athlete at Fairport High School. Bob went on to play baseball at Bucknell University, and he became a successful high school math teacher.

Bill Kreger—Shortstop/Outfield

Bill was an outstanding 3-sport and All-County athlete at East Rochester High School.

Bill played on the 1966 East Rochester, New York, Senior League World Champion baseball team. Bill then played baseball and football at Brockport State College.

Subsequently, Bill has enjoyed a successful career in sales and marketing.

Don Leege—Catcher/Infield/Outfield

Don was one of East Rochester's all-time finest athletes. Don starred in 3 sports while at East Rochester High School, earning multiple All-County awards. Don was a star member of the 1965 East Rochester, New York State Senior League Championship baseball team. Don went on to become one of the nation's leading catchers at Furman University. He was drafted by the San Diego Padres, and he played one year professionally. Subsequently, Don became a successful commercial banker, and an accomplished amateur golfer.

Chuck Glaza—Infield/Outfield/Catcher

Chuck was an outstanding, multisport athlete at Fairport High School. He was a steady and reliable hitter and fielder, and he contributed whenever and wherever he was needed. Chuck continues to be a successful Rochester-area businessman.

Rich Petersen—Catcher

Rich was one of Rush-Henrietta High School's top athletes, and a leader of the 1967 Ely Fagan State Championship team. As the team's starting catcher, Rich was a flawless fielder and a dependable, clutch hitter.

Ralph Clapp—Third Base and Team Co-Captain

Ralph was a 3-sport and All-County athlete at Rush-Henrietta High School. He was a team leader, played flawlessly at his third base position, and he hit for both high average and power. Ralph went on to become a star in baseball at Monroe Community College and Bowling Green State University. After college, Ralph became a leading Rochester-area teacher and coach, and he has subsequently received multiple teaching and coaching honors and Hall of Fame recognitions.

Rich Goodwin—First Base, Team Co-Captain, and Book Author

Other team contributors: Barb Petersen, Coach Petersen's daughter and head scorekeeper, and Tom Pannoni, and Al Goodwin, team batboys.

My Walk with Baseball

By Al Pannoni

Here are just some of Al Pannoni's sports and baseball accomplishments:

1. Played Little League Baseball from 1956–1961, at ages 8–12, in the 19th Ward in Rochester, mostly as a pitcher and infielder. Al's Little League experience was highlighted by winning the New York State Championship Tournament in 1961, playing on the Rochester Moose Baseball Team.
2. Played Pony League Summer Baseball in the 19th Ward from 1963–1965.
3. Played high school baseball at Rush-Henrietta from 1963–1966, and was selected to the first Team, Division I, All-County baseball team.
4. Played American Legion Baseball for the Ely Fagan Legion Team 1966–1967, with the 1967 team winning the New York State American Legion Baseball Championship.
5. Played centerfield for the Monroe Community College baseball team in 1967–1968, and legendary, nationally acclaimed coach, Dave Chamberlain, winning the 1967 Regional Championship, and being selected to the All-Conference team.
6. Played for the University of Buffalo baseball team from 1969–1970.

7. Taught physical education in Gates-Chili Central School District for 35 years, served as Football Coach for 32 years, and was inducted into the Section V Football Hall of Fame in 2010.

Here are a few of Al's thoughts about baseball and team chemistry:

About my coach, Dave Chamberlain, and Team Chemistry — Coach Chamberlain did an outstanding job of defining player roles. Players wanted and needed to know what to expect, and what he expected from them. Moreover, our Monroe Community College baseball team captains did an outstanding job of reinforcing player roles as well. Our team not only practiced baseball skills, but we also practiced "Team Chemistry" skills! Over the course of the season, our team chemistry helped propel us to another level — that of Region III Baseball Champions in 1967.

More on team chemistry — Team chemistry was essential to our team's success. Although our team chemistry was intangible, we knew we had it. We knew it was present when team members got along with each other, when we were loyal to each other, and when we worked toward the same goal. Essentially, our team chemistry arose from the qualities each team member contributed, and the supportive interactions team members had with each other. I felt our 1967 Monroe Community College team had just average talent. I thought we had a .500 team at best. However, what we lacked in talent, we made up for in team chemistry, and it was our team chemistry that made all the difference. Our players cared more about the team than individual success. Our players were comfortable warming up with different teammates, and not just their familiar friends. And we engaged in team activities off the field too, such as team dinners and going to movies together. The more interaction we had between players, the stronger the chemistry became, and the better we played on game days.

The 1961 New York State Championship Rochester Moose Baseball Team
Al Pannoni is kneeling front and center

GETTING STARTED IN BASEBALL

By Gary Junge

My first time playing baseball was when we moved from the city to Henrietta. I was 9 years old and was scared stiff of getting hit when batting, so I either walked or struck out! My dad took me aside and threw batting practice to me, and proceeded to hit me a few times, and that helped me to conquer my fear of getting hit by those wild pitches. I also had my first experience pitching, and I would either strike out the batter or walk him! There was no pitch count, so who knows how many pitches I actually threw in a 6-inning game.

My second year was much better, as I threw my first no-hitter and hit 3 home runs in that same game. I was rewarded with a small article in the newspaper the next day!

I played a few more years in youth baseball, and when I tried out for the freshman high school baseball team, I was not allowed to play because I wore braces on my teeth, and the local doctor told me no baseball until those braces came off. So, instead of being a player, I became the team manager.

My sophomore year, I played JV and continued pitching. My junior year, we had most of the varsity pitchers return, so I was sent down to pitch a JV game to get in some work. Unfortunately, out of nowhere, one of the starting pitchers on the varsity team sustained an injury. So, lo and behold, I was summoned up to pitch my first varsity game in his place! Well, it couldn't have been any sweeter because I threw a no-hitter and slammed a double in that first varsity game! From then on, I was undefeated at 6–0, and I was selected first team All-County.

In my senior high school year, my pitching record ended up being 9–4, and our team lost in the sectional finals 4–1 when the opposing team ended up winning by bunting us to death!

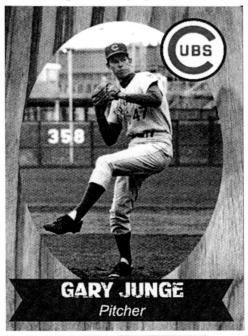

GARY JUNGE
Pitcher

GARY JUNGE

Ht: 6'3" • Wt: 190lb • Throws: Right • Bats: Right • Home: Henrietta, NY
Born: September 19, 1948, Rochester, NY • Full Name: Gary Steven Junge

PITCHING STATS

HITTING STATS

REFLECTIONS ABOUT A SUCCESSFUL JOURNEY IN BASEBALL

By Gary Junge

As I approached graduation from Rush-Henrietta Senior High School, while looking at colleges to attend, I didn't consider going south so I focused on schools in the Northeast. I did receive an offer from the University of Rochester, but only for $1,000 per year, while Clarkson University offered me full tuition, which was $1,700 for 4 years. Plus the Clarkson baseball coach had been a professional ballplayer, and I figured that could prove beneficial someday if I decided to pursue a professional baseball career. So, I pretty much decided I would attend Clarkson in New York State's North Country! I concluded the offer from Clarkson would be the better way to go. I ended up having a successful college career, and even pitched a no-hitter my senior year. I was hoping I'd be drafted right out of college, but I wasn't. So, I got together with my former high school coach and we sent letters to numerous professional scouts, and we told them I was looking for a tryout. It worked!

That summer I was invited to a tryout with Cincinnati, and I was subsequently offered $10,000 toward an additional college degree, but they didn't offer me a signing bonus. I wasn't sure if I did sign with Cincinnati, I would want to go back to college at some later date after my baseball playing days were over. I also went to a Pittsburgh tryout, but nothing came from that. After mailing the letters, I did get a response from the Chicago Cubs with a contract offer to report to spring training the next spring. Of course I jumped on the opportunity and signed the contract with no bonus, but at least a chance to play. I also received an offer from the Oakland A's, but by then I had already signed with the Cubs.

My first experience in spring training was a shocker. I pitched well and thought that I would go to AA or A that summer, but was told they had just disbanded one of their level A teams, so 25 extra players had to try out for the one A team that was left. Off I went to Quincy, Illinois, to practice for 8 weeks until the end of June, when I would go to Caldwell, Idaho, for rookie ball. However, the day I arrived in Quincy, a coach knocked on my hotel room door and said that my roommate and I were going to Chicago the next day to pitch batting practice for the Cubs! I spent the next 5 weeks with the big club in Chicago, and traveled to New York, Montreal, and Philadelphia, and was in heaven! Then, I was on to Idaho, where I was the fourth pitcher in the rotation to begin the season. Well, we lost the first 3 games when the pitchers that were drafted that spring got to start, and none of them faired very well. I pitched into the 7th inning, and we won the game 3–2. So I got the first, and only, win for the 5-game homestand, and got a hit, and scored a run to boot!

I thought I was on the way to great things only to be told a couple days later that I was in the bullpen for the rest of the year. As it turned out, the pitchers that they had the most money invested in became their starters. I found myself on the roster of the Minor League A level team the next year, and I pitched as a reliever and recorded 13 saves in Quincy. Then I was promoted to AA the following year, and they made me a starter! I finished 9–9 for a last-place team and was in the top 10 for the league starters in ERA. At that point, I figured I had a good chance to move up to AAA the next year, but instead I found myself back in AA. The next year I did move up to AAA for about 5 weeks, but only appeared in 3 games and was sent back to AA, where we won a championship. We had Bruce Sutter, Dennis Lamp, Mike Krukow, Donnie Moore, and Dave Geisel on the pitching staff, all of whom played several years in the Major Leagues. Bruce Sutter had a great Major League pitching career, and he was eventually inducted into the Baseball Hall of Fame.

My final year with the Cubs was again back in AA, and by that time I was married and had a baby girl. At that time, there was no free agency, but the Cubs did try to trade me to Cleveland, however, that trade fell through, so at the end of the year, I sat down with the general manager for Midland, and we decided that if I did not get a good opportunity to play at the AAA level the next year, I would retire and use my college degree to get a job back in Rochester. When I arrived home my release papers were already in the mailbox.

I thoroughly enjoyed my years with the Cubs and made many friends along the way, but my favorite memories were playing for Ely Fagan and winning the New York State Championship.

I continued to stay involved with baseball in Rush-Henrietta, and coached the Ely Fagan legion team for 9 years. I also became active in, and served, the RHAA—our town baseball program—for over 30 years.

Being inducted into the second class of the Section V Hall of Fame in 2012 was a special honor because I followed Rochester's greats, Johnny Antonelli, Bob Keegan, and Ed Nietopski, who were inducted in the first, inaugural class. But being inducted with my 1967 Ely Fagan teammates into Rochester's Walk of Fame, at Frontier Field in 2018, was the best of all. I was fortunate to have played with the most talented baseball players in the area, and we rarely lost a game. We won the Monroe County championship 3 consecutive years. Those teams, the players, and the baseball experiences we shared were some of the best memories in my life, and getting together again with the members of the 1967 team the past few years has been something I will never forget.

My Life in Baseball
and the Ely Fagan Team
By Ralph Clapp, Co-Captain and Third Baseman

Early Years

I was extremely fortunate to grow up in Henrietta, NY, in a family that was sports-oriented and especially interested in baseball and softball. Early memories include my father teaching me the finer points of hitting and fielding a baseball and softball. Over the years I have come to realize the influence my father had on me and our family, and how the games of baseball and softball were passed on to each successive generation as I now watch our grandsons enjoy playing them.

I played in the Rush-Henrietta Athletic Association Little League program, which was so instrumental in the early development of my baseball career. The RHAA remains strong today with the great leadership of people like Gary Junge, who has unselfishly contributed many years of dedicated service to this great organization!

High School and College

I was fortunate to play third base for the Rush-Henrietta, New York varsity baseball team under the guidance of our coach, Jack Smith. We were Section V semifinalists and finalists, and I was named to the All-Monroe County team in 1967, and in that same year, was a member of the Ely Fagan American Legion Team that won the New York State Championship.

After high school, I went on to attend Monroe Community College in Rochester, New York, where I played baseball for legendary coach Dave Chamberlain. Coach Chamberlain had the biggest influence on me as a person, and later, in helping me develop my coaching philosophy. I was so fortunate to have played in successful and outstanding baseball programs. They all shared the same important and fundamental philosophy of team first over individual achievements. I came to believe in that philosophy and understand good teams become great ones when the team members trust each other enough to surrender the "ME" for the "WE." Cal Ripkin, Sr. was quoted saying, "Everything that happens in baseball happens in life," and I have found that to be so true.

While at Monroe Community College, I was selected to the All-Regional team as a shortstop, as well as MVP in 1969, and 1970. I served as captain of the 1970 team and was inducted into the MCC Athletic Hall of Fame in 1984.

Bowling Green State University in Ohio was the next stop for me, where I played for a great coach, Don Purvis. As a senior I was named captain and voted MVP, and was selected to the Mid-American All-Conference Team.

CAREER

After graduating from college, I was fortunate enough to be hired to teach and coach baseball in the Rochester, New York, area; a career I enjoyed for over 35 years! In 1973, I returned to the Rush-Henrietta Central School District for 3 years before heading to Pittsford Mendon in 1976, where I spent 7 years as the JV Baseball Coach and 7 more years as the Varsity Baseball Coach. My final baseball teaching and coaching stint was at Honeoye Falls-Lima High School, where I spent 3 years at the JV level and 14 years at the varsity level, achieving a career coaching record of 226–76. My teams at Honeoye Falls-Lima earned 8 Livingston

County Division I titles and were Section V Finalists 5 times. I was named Livingston County Coach of the Year from 1998 to 2000, and Section V Coach of the Year in 1999 and 2003, and received The New York State Coaches Association Honor Award in 2001.

THE ELY FAGAN TEAM

When I reflect back on our Ely Fagan Championship season, I first think of Coach Harold Petersen, and the tremendous job he did in leading a group of young men from 3 different high schools to The New York State Championship in Cooperstown, New York, in 1967. As a baseball coach myself, I know the challenges of molding a team to get the right chemistry so that the players are on the same page; trying to sacrifice themselves for the good of the team. I felt this was one of Coach Petersen's greatest assets, as he taught us that the game should be played a certain way . . . play hard, always run on and off the field, and respect the game and your opponents. Winning that New York State Championship was a great accomplishment, and it gave me a lot of confidence as a baseball player, and as a person, moving forward in life.

The game of baseball has provided me with almost everything significant that I have accomplished in my life, including a great education that has allowed me to have a positive influence on the many students and athletes that I have taught and coached during my career.

I met my wonderful wife, Debra, at Bowling Green State University. She was a big fan of baseball and enjoyed watching the Bowling Green baseball games. We continue to enjoy our love of baseball, and we share many other common interests as well. She, too, was a physical education teacher and coach for many years. We have 3 wonderful children who, from an early age, had taken an avid interest in baseball and softball, and now have passed that love of the sport to their children. I cannot express how fortunate I have been to play the game that I genuinely love—baseball! All the great baseball-related friendships I have developed over the years along with the incredible coaches I have had, have deeply impacted my life.

In 2018 our American Legion Baseball team was selected for the Team of the Ages Award for the Frontier Field Walk of Fame in Rochester, New York.

BASEBALL LIFE MEMORIES

By Rene Piccarreto

My story starts well before our glorious summer of 1967, and has not yet ended. The winning of the American Legion State Championship in 1967 was truly a great summer adventure for my teammates and friends. The runs, hits, errors, wins, and losses are still seared in my memory of that championship game, and many others played in 1967, but they are not the most important part of the adventure. What remains are the life lessons learned, and lasting friendships with teammates. The adventure starts with our coach, Harold Petersen.

In 1965, I was having a pretty good year as a high school sophomore playing up on the Rush-Henrietta varsity baseball team. We had a pretty good team, and I played well. Occasionally, I was asked to pitch for the junior varsity team. Pitching however, was not really in my future. At the end of that season, Coach Harold Petersen told me that he did not have any room for me on his 1965 American Legion team. That was a crushing blow by the coach for me. During that summer, I played on the Intertown team, and we beat everybody in sight. Those teammates became part of the nucleus for the next 2 highly successful, Rush-Henrietta varsity baseball teams and the 1967 American Legion team. Coach Petersen had set in motion the foundation for those teams and future lifelong friendships. He also taught me a very important and positive lesson for life. Every failure in life is an opportunity to learn and improve!

This book would not be complete without a discussion about

our coach, Harold Petersen. Mr. Petersen was a no-nonsense guy. You played baseball his way, the right way, or you did not play. During WWII he served in the US Navy, as did many of our fathers and mothers. Coach Petersen was a Navy second-class machinist's mate aboard the USS Eagle. The Eagle was torpedoed in April of 1945, and it sank. Only 13 of the crew of 62 survived, including Mr. Petersen. For many years, the Navy insisted that the crew had made mistakes resulting in the boiler blowing up and causing the USS Eagle to sink. This contradicted the surviving crewmembers, who insisted and testified that, in fact, a German submarine had sunk the Eagle, and while in the freezing water, they spotted a submarine that had surfaced. In 2001, the Navy's record of events was changed because evidence came to light that a German submarine had indeed sunk the Eagle. Divers found the USS Eagle and noted that the hull had been penetrated from outside in and not blown inside out. Our coach was a survivor! In 2001, when I saw the article about the USS Eagle and Mr. Petersen, I thought that explained a lot about our coach, and how he acted, what he demanded from us, what he demanded from himself, and the example he set. Those lessons have served me well in my 70 years. Thanks Coach Petersen!

Some of the success of our 1967 team also goes to Bill Farrell. Mr. Farrell was the athletic director at Rush-Henrietta when I was a student there. Mr. Farrell was also the head of the Rush-Henrietta Youth Baseball program. In 1965, he changed the program format from being a traditional youth summer baseball program to an enhanced baseball program that provided the opportunity for junior varsity and varsity baseball players to become instructors and coaches. We had blue pants, white T-shirts, and baseball caps. We worked Monday through Friday. On Saturdays we went to Mr. Farrell's house where he would teach some aspect of baseball. Mr. Farrell had developed a notebook on every aspect of teaching the game of baseball. This notebook was far ahead of its time and had the effect of putting us way ahead in our knowledge of the game. At the end of the lesson, we would jump in his pool and play water polo. Those polo games provided a solid basis for team bonding which served us well. Those summers of learning how to teach and coach baseball provided me and my teammates with experience and knowledge about the game that was well ahead of any other baseball players in the area. We learned about preparation and attention to detail. Our experience as teachers and coaches of the game gave us a competitive edge in 1967. We might not have been as talented as other teams, but we had the knowledge to execute the game at a high level, considering our ages. Many of my teammates went on to be successful teachers and coaches. Ralph Clapp and Fred Pannoni went on to be highly successful teachers and coaches. Gary Junge has run the Rush-Henrietta Youth Baseball Program successfully for many years. Many of us became teachers, including Dick Goodwin and myself. I attribute some of my success to Mr. Bill Farrell and the lessons learned at a young age. Thanks Mr. Farrell!

Some of our memories from that summer of 1967 are extraordinary. We played a game in Bath, New York, at the VA complex. This was a complex for veterans to get needed services, and it also provided a large burial place for veterans. Prior to the game, there was a ceremony to honor a local resident who had recently been killed in Vietnam. During the ceremony, a large oak tree fell in right field. That was eerie! I was the right fielder, and special ground rules had to be made for right field so we could play around the tree. We played that game with that huge tree laying on the ground and won. I don't remember the score, or how we won, or what I did in that game, but I do remember the ceremony, the tree, and most importantly, the man who gave his life in service to our county. Up to that point, I had no notion that our people were fighting and dying in Vietnam. Message received! I learned there and then that there is a cost for all our freedoms.

On a much lighter note, these are some of the people who supported our team that summer: Barb Petersen comes to mind first. She kept the scorebook. You did not get a hit, error, or an RBI unless Barb thought so. She was fair but tough like her dad, Coach

Petersen. What is extraordinary about Barb is that she was, in her own right, a great, multisport athlete. She and my sister, Donna, played together on things called "playdays." These were events for girls that were held by the public schools. During the '60s there was no opportunity for girls to participate in individual or team sports. No Title 9! Barb might have been a better athlete than her brothers, who were great, multisport athletes, or any of my other teammates. Barb and Donna seemed to beat everybody, in every sport. Barb was a good scorekeeper, but a better lifelong friend.

We had batboys who travelled with us. Dick Goodwin's bother, Al, and Al Pannoni's brother, Tom, were our batboys. Who has batboys in American Legion Baseball? We did, and they were great! Our team, at the time, probably had little idea about their presence during games, but as adults we have come to realize and recognize that they contributed to our team's success, and they have been part of our team reunions ever since.

Our parents were great supporters of our team. They got us to practice, purchased our equipment, and went to every game. My father taught me how to hit. On weekends he would pitch to me, and teach me how to hit, throw, and field. He was demanding! After every game, there was the "Review of the Game." Even if I was 4 for 4, the review was always about what I didn't do or should have done. He was always proud of me. My mother went to every game. She endured snow, rain, heat, cold, and wind. She was always there cheering the team and me on. I remember a game at the East Ridge High School field, and at that time I was in 7th grade. It was raining, and I was pitching. "Pitching" is a loose translation for what I was doing. In 4 innings I managed to walk 16 players! My mother was parked in a car overlooking the field, and through the whole rainy, cold game, I could hear her cheering me and my team on. Mom was always positive, supportive, and always there. My girlfriend during those high school years was Pat. She became my wife, and she was a great supporter. She would help me become a better hitter. Pat would pitch tennis balls from 20 feet, and I would try to hit them with a broomstick in my backyard. She was another good athlete who did "playdays," but never got to demonstrate her athletic ability until later in life. These days she scuba dives, plays golf, and walks half marathons.

The championship game at Cooperstown's Doubleday Field was the best game I was ever in. Gary Junge pitched 12 innings of scoreless ball, as did the pitcher from Staten Island. They gave up few hits, fewer walks, and no serious scoring opportunities. Gary threw a great fastball that was always knee high, and it moved as it traveled toward batters. He went on to play professionally. I'm sure he could have gone a few more innings in the championship game. Gary did not need a pitch count the way pitchers do today. He could just throw hard, inning after inning. The hotter the weather, the better Gary was. By the bottom of the 12th, both starting pitchers had to be replaced due to inning restrictions. In the top of the 13th, Andy Haefner came in to pitch. Andy threw 9 pitches and the inning was over. He struck out everybody! Each hitter saw 3 pitches—all strikes and then they sat down. Andy had a good fastball and a great curve. When his curve was going, Andy was unhittable. If that game had gone more innings, we still would have won because nobody from Staten Island was going to hit Andy that day. Staten Island did not know that at the top of the 13th, but by the bottom of the 13th they knew how tough he was. In the bottom of the 13th, Bobby Porta was walked and stood safely on first base. Bobby tragically died early in life from a brain tumor. Bobby was a quiet guy, but a good 2nd baseman, good leadoff hitter, and a great teammate. I was next up and pulled a pitch into the right field corner. What is odd, is that I usually NEVER pulled baseballs much. My style, if you can call it a style, was inside out. Derek Jeter made that style famous during his career with the Yankees. Most of my hits were from center field to left field direction. The table was now set with no outs and guys on second and third. After a fly out, our 4th hitter in the lineup was Dick Goodwin. They walked Dick. Dick was one of the best hitters I ever played with and against. He played college ball at

Ithaca College and was a great hitter there. He could hit anything and usually did. Staten Island wanted no part of Dick, and walked him on 4 pitches. Joe Baldassare was next up, and he hit a clean single to right center field to score Bobby Porta, and we won in walk-off fashion! Unfortunately, Joe also passed early in life like Bobby Porta. I often think about how fortunate some have been in life and how others weren't.

After we went to Cooperstown and won the New York State Championship, then we were off to New Jersey to vie for the Regional American Legion Championship. The place was Bordentown, New Jersey. It was close to the famous boardwalk and Jersey shore. We got there and beat the host team soundly on the first day. On the last day there, we lost a close game to the New Jersey State champs, and they went on to the national tournament. In between, it rained and rained and rained! At one point, an Army helicopter was brought in to blow the water off the field. I don't remember much about the games, although I do remember hitting a home run in one of them. That home run was memorable because I was your basic singles hitter. The hit was a towering fly that easily cleared the fence in right center. Usually, I hit home runs when there was no fence, and the ball just rolled and rolled into a gap in left or right center. Any other day it would have been a double or triple in a field without a fence. What was most memorable, though, was the rain and boredom between games throughout the week we were there.

During the recent summer of 2018, our team was honored as a Team of the Ages with a brick that is now part of the "Walk of Fame" at Rochester's Frontier Field—the home to the International League professional baseball team, the Rochester Red Wings. The honor was a long time coming—51 years. No other team from Monroe County has ever won the New York State American Legion Championship. Gary Junge and Dick Goodwin are largely responsible for this honor, and I am grateful and indebted to them for their efforts on behalf of my teammates and myself. At the 2018 ceremony, the team met at the stadium, and we were served a delicious lunch. After lunch, our brick was officially placed in the

"Walk of Fame" section of Frontier Field. We were introduced to the crowd, and then we watched a Red Wings game together. Then, after the game, the Ely Fagan American Legion Post hosted us for a celebration. It was a fun day. The Ely Fagan Post has, over the years, hosted the team gatherings, and that is much appreciated. Gary Junge brought out some of our old uniforms from our historic 1967 season. Wow! Those uniforms were wool, heavy, hot, and scratchy. Thankfully we never noticed or cared about that because we were all about playing baseball.

Our time as baseball players has long since passed. I love to watch games and go out with my grandsons to the batting cages to take swings. Our legacy is a bunch of kids from Rush-Henrietta, East Rochester, and Fairport who came together as a team, played the game right, played at a very high level, and won a state championship. We did that with guidance from people like Harold Petersen, our coach, and Bill Farrell, team manager and mentor. We did that with support from parents and loved ones. We were young, tough, resilient, and loved the game of baseball. I will forever be grateful to my teammates for the games we played as kids and the lifetime of friendships that continue to this day! Ely Fagan and our 1967 baseball season was a great adventure, and the adventure continues when we get together as teammates and friends to share our life experiences with one another!

THE 1967 AMERICAN LEGION REGION II BASEBALL PLAYOFFS

After winning the 1967 New York State American Legion Baseball Championship, Ely Fagan went on in late August to represent Rush-Henrietta, the Greater Rochester, NY, area, and New York State in the Region II Baseball Playoffs. The winner of this competition would then travel to Memphis, Tennessee, and compete for the national title!

Held at BORDENTOWN, NJ, on Gilder Field

THE TEAMS

Ely Fagan Post #1151 from Rush-Henrietta, New York—New York State Champions

Parkersburg Post #15 from Parkersburg, West Virginia—West Virginia State Champions

Cheverly Post #108 from Cheverly, Maryland—Maryland State Champions

Joseph B. Stahl Post #30 from Wilmington Manor, Delaware—Delaware State Champions

Hamilton Post #31 from Hamilton Township/Trenton, New Jersey—New Jersey State Champions

Adelphia Post #38 from Washington, DC—District of Columbia Champions

Ervin V. Hamilton Post #26 from Bordentown, New Jersey—Home Team Selection

*Torrential rains resulted in unplayable field conditions, and 3 consecutive days of postponement of games.

1967 REGION 2 TOURNAMENT
AMERICAN LEGION BASEBALL
GILDER FIELD, BORDENTOWN, N. J.

Ely Fagans Post #1151
Henrietta, New York

Uniform No.	Name	Position
10.	Dick Goodwin	1B
11.	Rich Peterson	C
12.	Rene Piccarreto	OF
13.	Al Pannoni	SS
15.	Gary Junge	P
18.	Don Leege	IF-OF
19.	Andy Haefner	P
20.	Joe Haefner	OF
22.	Bob Porta	2B
24.	Ralph Clapp	3B
25.	John Kokinda	P OF
	Bill Kreger	IF
	Joe Baldassare	OF P
	Harold Peterson	mgr.

Hamilton Post #31
Hamilton Township, N.J.

Uniform No.	Name	Position
1.	Dick Schnell	P
3.	Bruce Gorland	OF
4.	Frank Fratarangeli	2B
5.	Gary Hohman	C
6.	Ed Terlecki	OF
7.	Bob herrara	1B
8.	Tom Bartolone	OF-C
9.	Rich Mallam	3B
10.	Lee Jackson	P
11.	Dave Powell	1B
12.	Bill Povia	SS
13.	Bob Petrino	P-OF
14.	Fred Armenti	P-OL
15.	Wolfgang Van Kornya	OF
	Pat Petrino	coach
	Vito Petrino	coach
	Clarence Ahr	mgr.

Joseph B. Stahl Post #30
Wilmington Manor, Delaware

Uniform No.	Name	Position
1.	Robert Riley	IF
3.	Joseph Cherico	IF-P
4.	John Leeman	OF-C
5.	Frederick Bloom	IF-OF
6.	Gregory Simendinger	P-OF
7.	John May	OF-IF
8.	Robert Scott	C-OF
9.	Randall Nowell	C
10.	Stephen Nepa	P-IF
11.	Raymond Justison	IF-OF
12.	James Robinson	IF
13.	Douglas Hopper	P-OF
15.	Vincent McMahon	OF-P
16.	Eugene Flickinger	coach
17.	Charles Rynkowski	P-OF
18.	George Benson	coach
22.	Ronald Benson	batboy

Cheverly Post #108
Cheverly, Maryland

Uniform No.	Name	Position
20.	Mike Lancaster	3B
21.	Kirk Lovall	OF
22.	Bill Hegland	P
23.	Glenn Fry	SS
24.	Joe Kaub	P
25.	Charles Slifko	OF
26.	Craige Smith	C
27.	Fred Koennel	P
28.	Paul Stombaugh	P
29.	Bill Collins	C
30.	Tom Graham	OF
31.	Bill Hunter	OF
32.	Dennis Butner	P
34.	Steve Garrett	2B
35.	John Jones	P
38.	James German	C
	William Vaughn	mgr.
	Robert Burkart	coach

Adelphia Post #38
Washington, D.C.

Name	Position
Dan Parker	IF
Jim Boyd	IF-P
Danny Bryan	IF
Ed Gibbs	IF
Charles Kendall	P
John Krug	IF
Dave Lenney	P
Doug Lloyd	OF
Larry Mallam	P
David Nagy	P
Lee Richardson	IF
Bill Seyford	OF
Bill Stoyer	P-OF
Willie Wood	OF
Dave Zenns	C
Jake Jacobs	mgr.

Parkersburg Post #15
Parkersburg, W. Va.

Uniform No.	Name	Position
5.	Robert Wentzel	C
6.	Richard Deleney	3B
9.	Richard DeQuasie	LF
14.	Daniel Bucca	P
15.	Nathaniel Ayre	SS
16.	Terrel Jones	P
18.	Michael Boice	coach
20.	Michael Smith	1B
22.	Joseph Robrecht	2B
24.	Wade Wileen	P
25.	Steven Swisher	P
26.	David Eaton	C
27.	Joseph DeHaven	RF
28.	Fred BOICE, mgr	CF
29.	Claude Beach, coach	mgr.

Ervin V. Hamilton #26
Bordentown, New Jersey

Uniform No.	Name	Position
1.	Kevin O'Connor	IF P
2.	Roland 'Gee' Wilkins	OF
3.	James Tucillo	OF
4.	Baldo Sebastenelli	IF P
5.	Alan Cox	P
6.	Neil Moore	IF-P
7.	George Carmichael	C
8.	Terry Ryle	IF-P
9.	Gary Begnaud	IF
10.	Kermit Pigott	IF
11.	Joseph Malone Jr.	C
13.	James Nemeth	P
15.	Richard Mathews	IF
30.	Dick Duddy	OF-IF
32.	Toby Sutton	IF
	Byron Crammer	coach
20.	William McDonough	mgr.

Ely Fagan won 2 games—defeating the Parkersburg, West Virginia team and the team from Bordentown, New Jersey—but was ultimately eliminated and did not move on to the American Legion National Tournament held in Memphis, Tennessee. The 1967 National Champion was the Tuscaloosa, Alabama Post #34 team which defeated the Northbrook, Illinois Post #791 team.

1967 Ely Fagan Region II Tournament Winning Pitchers:

Andy Haefner AND Joe Baldassare

The team then returned home to capture the Monroe County/Rochester-area American Legion Baseball Championship which was played on the historic Red Wing Stadium field.

SO WHAT ELSE IS NEW? — County Times photographer Alex Zidock was on hand at Bordentown's Gilder Field yesterday as the rains hit the American Legion tourney for the fourth straight day. Only one game was completed before the storm struck, dropping the tournament even further back of its original schedule. "The heavy rain flooded the playing area making today's schedule a questionable one once again. (Times Sports Photo by Zidock)

The rain-drenched Gilder Field

FOCUS

By Rene Piccarreto

I had a terrible fall season of 1967, when I first played baseball at The University of Arizona, after our historic Ely Fagan victory in August on Cooperstown's Doubleday Field. That following winter, I worked on my hitting with a relief pitcher for the Cleveland Indians who wanted to get ready for his upcoming 1968 baseball season. He threw left-handed, and after facing him over time, I learned to keep my right shoulder in. That practice with him helped me figure it out, and I became a much more effective hitter against left-handed pitchers. The key, as I learned, was to watch the ball as it came out of the pitcher's hand instead of watching the leg kick and other movements, which were designed to distract me from focusing on the thrown ball. Becoming more disciplined and learning to focus on the thrown ball instead of pitcher's distractors made all the difference for me!

My ability to focus improved tremendously when I was in flight school while serving in the Marine Corps. We were drilled often on emergency procedures until it became natural to focus on the immediate problem or threat, solve it, and then to move on to the next problem. I learned how to prioritize the problem or threat, analyze it, and then solve it. I learned how to concentrate solely on that one thing, and at the same time, I learned how to block out the distractors.

I was taking off from Navy-Jacksonville when a U joint that held the steering cables failed as we were getting airborne. The joint collapsed onto the steering cables. The result was I had no up or down movement in the flight stick. I needed to yaw the aircraft using only the rudder to steer the plane. We declared an emergency! On the short, final approach back (at 50 feet), a fire engine crossed in front of me, and I had to go around, which was very dangerous considering I had no stick and needed to yaw the plane using the rudders. Anyway, I came around and landed safely! My ability to focus saved my life as well as the life of my bombardier navigator (BN). My BN was clearly upset, and he became frantic about our predicament and wanted to eject, but thankfully he didn't need to! Yes, the ability to focus has served me well!

Don Leege's
Baseball Journey

Don is from the little, upstate village of East Rochester, New York, and he grew up in a sports-minded family. His lovely mom knew lots about all sports (as did Don's 3 younger sisters), especially the ones Don played most—baseball, football, and wrestling. Don and I played on the same baseball teams in Little League, Senior League, high school, and we played on the Ely Fagan American Legion teams. After graduating from high school, Don played sports and studied business at Staunton Military Academy. Then he enrolled at Furman University/Southern Conference where he played baseball for 4 years. During those 4 years, he had 3 different coaches with 3 different coaching philosophies, and the Furman teams had mediocre won-loss records, but despite that, Don excelled and set a number of hitting and fielding records.

Don started catching in Little League, and he credits his knowledgeable coach and father, Don Leege, Sr., with teaching him the fundamentals of catching and the game of baseball in general. But Don also learned to play other positions. He pitched, played third base, and he even played in the outfield from time to time. Our Little League team was a big winner, and it came within just several games of qualifying to go on to play in the Little League World Series in Williamsport, Pennsylvania, and Don's 1965 Senior League team won the New York State Championship. Our high school baseball team won the Rochester-Monroe County East AA Title in 1967, and then Don went on that summer to become part of the 1967 New York State Ely Fagan American Legion Championship team.

Scouts knew about Don when he arrived to play baseball at Furman. Some scouts had seen him play, and he already had a reputation for being a fine, right-handed hitter—a consistent hitter with a quick bat and some power—and also for being an outstanding catcher with a strong and accurate throwing arm. Yes, not many baserunners dared to try to steal a base against Furman when Don was catching behind the plate! For the most part, baserunners who did steal bases when Don caught did so because they got huge leads, so they really stole bases on the pitcher, not on Don. Scouts saw that, and scouts knew that, and it was a big reason why Don was so highly sought after by professional baseball teams.

After graduating from Furman, Don was drafted as a catcher by the San Diego Padres organization—which made his mom and dad very happy—and he was off to the west coast to play. As a rookie, Don found himself among many young, baseball-playing hopefuls, including his first roommate, Kurt Russell . . . the actor Kurt Russell! Yes, Kurt Russell was a talented baseball player, in addition to being a terrific actor and entertainer! In a night game, as Don told the story years later, Don was catching, and this young, right-handed hitter came to the plate. In came the pitch and the hitter swung, the ball was hammered and launched high and far up over the left field fence, and it disappeared far into the night's darkness up and beyond the field lights. Don estimated the ball traveled around 450 feet! Who was the hitter? It was a young, strong Chet Lemon who went on to have an illustrious Major League career. Don ended up playing one season of pro ball because he sustained a broken hand in one of his games, and that injury, as it turned out, ultimately ended his pro career. Don was a fierce competitor, and he always played to win!

Our National Pastime

Football is exciting, it's fast moving, and it's brutal. Players hit other players hard, oftentimes hurting each other, and the offensive and defensive plays seem lightning quick at times. Size, speed, and quickness. That's football. Basketball is more a skills type game. Shoot the ball into the basket, and you score. It doesn't hurt that players are really tall and can dunk the ball by merely hopping up and reaching toward the rim. For taller players, it truly is a slam dunk! Basketball players are amazing athletes, in super shape, and they can run, run, run! But baseball has 9 innings of pitching, catching, hitting, fielding, throwing, and running, and sometimes games yield extra innings . . . a fan's delight! Hits come in all sorts of shapes and sizes. Hits can be long ones, short ones, high or low, they can be launched into the air, or they can hug the ground with big, small, and medium-sized bounces. Hits can be accidental or purposeful. Catches can be easy or difficult or somewhere in between, catches can be lucky, and catches can truly be unbelievable! Throws can be easy, hard or fast, wild or accurate, high or low, and throws can hit the target or miss the target, causing excitement in either case. There just isn't anything quite like the game of baseball, and that's why it has been, and will always be, our "National Pastime."

1949

Most of the 1967 Ely Fagan players were born in 1949. Of course, these baby boomers had no idea baseball would become a big part of their lives going forward. What was America and the world like back in 1949? Well, it's fair to say the world back then was considerably different than the life they grew into in 1967.

In 1949, Harry Truman was serving as our nation's 33rd president along with his vice-president, Alben Barkley. NATO came to being, and Mao Zedong became chairman of the People's Republic of China. Albert Einstein published his gravitation theory, and in the movies, the best actor award went to Broderick Crawford for his role in the movie, *All the King's Men*. A few of the popular songs included "Diamonds are a Girl's Best Friend," "Some Enchanted Evening," and "Rudolph the Red-Nosed Reindeer." Guy Lombardo was a hit as was Pard dog food! On the average, new houses cost around $7,000, new cars were around $1,500, and annual incomes were around $3,000. People were expected to live approximately 63 years.

In sports, boxing legend Joe Louis retired, Notre Dame's Leon Hart won the Heisman Trophy, the Toronto Maple Leafs won professional hockey's Stanley Cup, the Boston Marathon champ was Karl Lendersson, with a time of around 2½ hours, and professional baseball's World Series champs were the New York Yankees, managed by the great Hall of Famer Casey Stengel. Mr. Stengel was quoted saying, "I was not successful as a ball player as it was a game of skill." Of course, he was in fact an excellent baseball player, having played in the big leagues 14 years, and having amassed over 1,000 hits with a career batting average of over .280.

PLAYING
BASEBALL IN THE 1950S

As we all know, immediately after winning WWII, American soldiers returned home victorious and with high hopes for a brighter future, eager to plug back into society and begin their lives anew. It was a time for national celebration and thanksgiving, a time to reconnect with family and loved ones. There was a strong national sentiment, a sense of community, and yes, it was the time when the "baby boom" began! Families sprung up everywhere across the nation, and parents with children wanted them to grow up in a world of peace, and also to have a productive, healthy, and prosperous life.

Baseball was our "National Pastime," and more boys started to play in the Little League program. Parents, volunteers, and communities supported their Little League programs. They flourished across America! Playing baseball and playing Little League Baseball was woven into our sports culture, and it was the thing to do. That was back then, and of course today both boys and girls have many more options as to what they want to do and how they want to spend their summers.

Back then in cities and suburbs, free and unstructured play outdoors during summer recess from school was commonplace. Boys and girls hopped on our bikes and would ride or walk to friends' houses, or go to town, or go to parks and game fields, or would ride our bikes wherever we wanted to. Kids gained a sense of self-reliance, independence, and confidence, and we decided what to do, and where and when we would do it. It was safe because neighbors cared about us, and kept their eyes on us, and got involved whenever they needed to. Communities were cohesive and caring, and they supported their Little League programs and players.

We players learned good sportsmanship. Our coaches and parents taught us. We learned how to play by the rules.

IT'S THE LITTLE
THINGS THAT MATTER

I played first base from the time I started in Little League until the time I finished college play, graduated from college, got married, and enlisted in the US Army. After marriage and the US Army, my days of playing competitive baseball were over. I was contacted by the Montreal Expos and Detroit Tigers, and I was invited to several tryouts, but my wife and I decided not to pursue pro ball, instead agreeing on a different direction and career path. Besides, although a couple of scouts said they liked the way I played, they and I knew I was undersized to play the first base position. And I never learned how to play outfield. In retrospect, as a lefty, that probably would have been a good idea since there just weren't lots of 5-foot, 9-inch first basemen playing pro ball, but there were some left-handed 5-foot, 9-inch outfielders who had played pro ball. I remember one scout came up to me after an American Legion Baseball game and said, "You're a very good player—you just need to grow another 6 inches!" Easier said than done.

I was taught to play first base one way. I was taught and told to never let a ground ball get through me or past me. From the time I was 8 years old, I was taught and told to get my body in front of ground balls, and to get down low and stop ground balls. I was told to never ever let a ground ball go through my legs, or bounce over me or my mitt, or go around me. Keep the ball in front of me at all times; keep the ball in play. My body ended up with bumps and bruises, but the ball didn't get past me. Ever. In game situations, and in the 14 years I played organized and competitive baseball, I don't recall ever letting a ground ball get past me . . . under my mitt . . . through my legs. Now, did batted balls ever make their way between me and the second baseman? Sure, if they were hit hard enough and in the right place. But I was quick, and covered my first base area well, guarded against ground ball errors, and stopped balls traveling toward the outfield. I knew what to do, and how, and when to do it. Similarly, I was told and taught that all infielder throws—in the dirt to me at first base—were either to be caught, or blocked by my body in order to keep the ball in front of me and hence, in play. Just a few infielder throws got past me, escaping my mitt and body, although some went soaring over my head!

The point is I did what I needed to do. Always. I never forgot the fundamentals of playing first base. I pretty much mastered playing first base, and remembered not to allow myself to get "fancy" playing the position. I never took any ground balls or infielder thrown balls traveling over to me at first base for granted. Not that there weren't routine ground balls and infielder throws. There were plenty of those. But I didn't take shortcuts, and didn't assume the ground balls and infielder throws would do what they appeared they would do as they came my way.

Infield ground balls can sometimes take super "bad" unexpected hops, and sometimes some of those ground balls just can't be stopped. But just sticking the mitt out to catch the ball oftentimes isn't good enough. The mitt alone doesn't always catch or stop the ball. It takes the full commitment of the mitt and the body, whenever that's possible. Knocking the ball down, recovering and picking up the ball, and throwing it to make the play and prevent an error, and further complications, is the way to go. There are plenty of infielders who didn't and wish they could get another chance.

So, maybe to some this is a lot said about a little thing to do. But baseball—like life—is full of "little things" to do. Doing little things the right way, consistently, often is the difference between winning and losing, success or failure. In short, after all is said and done, maybe "it really is the little things that matter most."

41

Kent Scriber   Paul Patterson

Bob Borowicz   Rich Goodwin   Dom Gaudioso

PLAYING BASEBALL AT ITHACA COLLEGE

Sometime during my senior year of public high school, I was called into the guidance counselor's office. I didn't know why until I got there. He told me to sit down, and he asked me whether or not I planned to attend college after graduating from high school. I told him, "Yes," and he then asked me, "Where do you want to go and what do you want to study?" I was undecided but said I had some interest in business, and I mentioned I was interested in playing baseball. So, he came up with several places to consider, and I ended up attending Ithaca College. Back then, Ithaca was considered to be an expensive college. Yes, it was around $3,000 per year (and that cost was pretty much guaranteed for all 4 years), and it included tuition, room and board, and several additional perks. That was in 1967. Looking back, and compared to today's college and university costs, we sure got lots for our money at Ithaca College!

At Ithaca, I tried out for the freshmen team (at that time, freshmen were ineligible to play varsity), made the team, and started at first base. It was fun, and we played at some interesting places. When we played Cornell University's team at Cornell, I walked onto the old, historic Cornell baseball field and realized I was playing on a field where the great Hall of Famer Lou Gehrig played while at Columbia University many years before me. It was truly an honor to be and play there.

We also used the large, indoor Cornell field house for late winter/early spring indoor baseball practices, and that was very appreciated because it got us out of the typically cold, rainy, blustery Ithaca weather. The weather was always a factor in Ithaca. In fact, you could look outside on a chilly game day morning in May and see the baseball field was snow covered! And the month of May was the END of our baseball season, and well before the warm, sunny Ithaca weather settled in.

Playing baseball at Ithaca gave me a valuable opportunity to be part of fine teams of great guys and talented baseball players. That group of fine players included: Kent Scriber, Geoff Wright, Paul Patterson, Richie Miller, Dale Dirk, Craig Paterniti, Jon Speich, Jerry Gardner, Bob Borowicz, Ray "Skip" Borowicz, Rick Vogel, Dom Gaudioso, Sandy Overton, Keith Kurowski, and Tony Vizzie. Several are members of the Ithaca College Athletics Hall of Fame, and Patterson, Paterniti, Dirk, Wright, Goodwin, Miller, Bob, and "Skip" Borowicz, and Gaudioso, and others either played professional baseball, signed professional baseball contracts, or were invited to professional tryouts. Playing baseball at Ithaca College also provided chances to challenge myself further, to improve as a player, and to compete against some fine Division I and Division II players and teams.

Our varsity head coach was Carlton "Carp" Wood. I'm told he was bestowed the nickname "Carp" because he was such an avid fisherman. He attended Ithaca College as a student, excelled in sports, and played baseball for legendary coach, James "Bucky" Freeman. Ultimately, Coach Wood became a Hall of Fame college baseball coach. He also coached soccer and basketball successfully while at Ithaca College, and he was inducted as a charter member into the inaugural class of the Ithaca College Athletics Hall of Fame in 1969. He served his country courageously in the US Army during WWII, and he was awarded the Bronze Star. After the war, he played Minor League professional baseball in the New York Yankees organization for several years. He fielded well, and hit over .300. I found that Coach Wood was a man of few words. We rarely talked, and in the 3 years I played for him, we may have exchanged a total of 50 words between us. I find that incredible when I think about it now. I rarely heard Coach Wood say, "Nice play or good hit!" to me or to other players.

Looking back at those 3 years I played for him, and remembering I hit at a consistently high level, delivered some timely game-winning hits, scored some game-winning runs, and proved to be a record-setting fielder of my position, I find it odd. As a player, I initially wondered why, but eventually just went about my business to help the team win games. I came to accept it was just his way. Coach Wood was frugal. Our baseball program didn't have lots of money, so the coach tried to get the most from the modest amount of money he had at his disposal. We wore the same old, tattered "woolies" that previous players had worn years before, and my girlfriend and future wife, Judy, found herself often stepping in to mend my uniform rips and tears as they occurred along the way. And Coach Wood didn't like it when the bats broke. No, he didn't like it because when our bats cracked, it resulted in bat replacement, an additional expense for the baseball program. So, he thought he would save some money by switching our ash wood bats to hickory and maple bats, thinking they would be more resilient, durable, and less likely to crack or split. The concern about that was some hitters preferred the ash wood bats over the hickory and maple bats because the ash bats felt lighter and hitters preferred them, their overall feel, and the bat speed they could generate using them.

Thinking back, I'm surprised he didn't ask us to weave our own uniforms and cut trees to whittle our own bats during the off-season as additional ways to save even more money. Just kidding! Coach Wood was all business. I rarely saw a lighter side of the coach, although I did see him surrender a slight, brief smile on rare occasions. He was always focused before, during, and after games, and he offered little time for what could be considered small talk.

The coach had talented players. Most of his players came from New York State, and they were very good. He was especially blessed with outstanding pitchers, like Paul Patterson, Rick Vogel, Craig Paterniti, and Tony Vizzie, along with one of the very best defensive catchers in college baseball—Dom Gaudioso. Dom Gaudioso didn't make errors. He didn't allow passed balls. He didn't make throwing errors. As a matter of fact, all opposing teams and baserunners knew about Dom. Baserunners knew they would be thrown out if they tried to steal a base against Dominick Gaudioso. Consequently, they didn't even try to steal bases against us or Dom. After graduating from Ithaca, Dom played professional baseball for several years, and even spent a season as the bullpen catcher for the Chicago Cubs. Because of our dominant pitching, and our dominant catcher, and because of our decent hitting and fielding, we won most of our regular season games, and we represented our District in 3 consecutive NCAA Collegiate Division East Regional tournaments.

The coach sat in the front of the bus, and his spirited players sat behind him. Our bus trips to games were filled with fun, laughter, friendly banter, storytelling, card playing, fellowship, and camaraderie. Whether we were on the road to play Villanova, Penn State, Colgate, The University of Rochester, Seton Hall, Fairleigh Dickinson, Old Dominion, East Carolina, Buffalo University, or traveling to our numerous other game destinations, including NCAA Regional competitions in Virginia where we played against Stetson University, Florida Southern, or Springfield College, each bus trip was an adventure filled with spontaneity and entertainment. Sometimes I wonder how the coach endured all the noise and fun and excitement that took place behind him on the longer bus trips. Of course, we players eventually tired and slept, so there were some quiet times too. He didn't interfere when we were on the bus or on the field. He let us play, and he tried to give us a framework for success best he could. He was a student of the game of baseball, he knew what to do, and he gave us the chance to play.

We, his former players, are grateful for the opportunity he gave us to play and prove ourselves on the baseball field. Coach Wood seemed friendlier later on. Some years later, after coach retired, my wife, son, and I attended an Ithaca College reunion, and saw the coach walking around and mingling with alums and friends of his. He saw us, we walked up to him, and he recognized me, and was so gracious! He actually seemed happy to see me, my wife, and my young son. His blue eyes sparkled, he smiled, he talked, he seemed relaxed, and he showed interest in how we were doing. I was happy to see him, and surprised by his change in behavior. I thought to myself, "Is this the same man?" Shortly after, we attended a football game and ran into him again. Sure enough, he was friendly again and seemed happy to see me. Out of nowhere he said to me, "Hey, I want you to meet someone!" He put his arm around me and turned me toward a man standing near us. Then he introduced me to him.

"Rich, I'd like you to meet Eddie Sawyer." I said, "Pleased to meet you, Mr. Sawyer." Then, Coach insisted we take a picture together, and so we did. It happened very fast, and it was totally unexpected and amazing. Eddie Sawyer played baseball at Ithaca College, he is also in the Ithaca Athletics Hall of Fame, he played pro ball, and became a successful Major League Baseball manager, and National League Manager of the Year, and the successful manager of the 1950 National League Champion Philadelphia Phillies team known as the "Whiz Kids." What an unexpected treat it was to see Coach and meet Eddie Sawyer. I came to realize the coach knew baseball, he was task oriented, he did the best he could, and his retirement from teaching and from coaching seemed to really, really agree with him! After Coach Wood retired, Ithaca College named George Valesente the head baseball coach, and with that, the Ithaca College tradition of baseball excellence continued under his new and outstanding leadership. Over his 41 years as head baseball coach at Ithaca College, Coach "Val," along with his dedicated assistant coaches Frank Fazio, Geoff Wright, and others, and his fine players, won 2 Division III National Championships, the first in 1980, and the second in 1988. Hall of Fame Coach Valesente retired in 2020 after amassing over

1,100 wins, and his head coaching position was then passed into the very capable hands of his son, David Valesente. The Ithaca College tradition of baseball excellence now continues under David's leadership.

The decade of the 1960s was a challenging and tumultuous time for many Americans. We lost our president, his brother, and Martin Luther King, Jr. to assassination. The Vietnam War proved divisive, splitting families and institutions. And like all prior wars, the Vietnam War resulted in thousands of lives lost. Civil rights issues were front and center. New and exciting music came from across the Atlantic Ocean in the form of the Beatles and other British rock groups, and that music migration was referred to by some as a "British invasion." There was the historic Woodstock music festival, and much more. There is no question those years were an exciting, difficult, challenging, and uncertain time to live. But through it all, and during decades before and after, the game of baseball was there for fans and players alike. It helped provide a familiar, welcoming face to our society, as well as a much needed and appreciated sense of stability for both players and fans across America.

Coach Wood, Eddie Sawyer, and Rich Goodwin

Rich Goodwin, Frank Fazio, George Valesente, and Geoff Wright

WERE THEY REALLY
BETTER THAN WE WERE?

Growing up in the northeast in the 1950s–1960s, and playing baseball in the northeast, we learned early on that "baseball weather" usually didn't begin and settle in until the school year ended, toward the end of June, first part of July, and then it lasted until the end of August, first part of September, when the new school year began. So, essentially, nice weather baseball . . . when it was warm to hot, and sunny . . . usually lasted around 2 months! Yes, while in school, we practiced baseball starting in February and March in cold, blustery, windy, wet, rainy, cloudy outdoor conditions when we could, along with our "weather controlled" indoor, gym practices.

On the average, players of baseball from the south had a distinct advantage of enjoying extended warmer, sunnier weather in the spring, summer, and fall seasons. They could begin and continue their play of baseball in "baseball-suitable" weather for longer periods of time. But were those players better players than their northern counterparts who had poorer weather and a shorter baseball season?

Southern players had more time to practice, more time to hold games, more time and opportunity to improve their playing skills and performances. When you factor in the extra time for practice and game playing, I guess you could make the case, "Yes, southern players were, and are better." However, if you subtract that extra time for practice and game playing (that was and still is climate dependent) from the equation, a case could also be made that "No, players from the south really weren't (and aren't) better at all." I guess that can be shown by tracking northern players of baseball who went south to play junior college baseball, college and university baseball, and flourished in that southern environment. Having more time and the opportunity to play baseball resulted in former northern players improving their base skills and performances to the same levels of their southern player levels.

So, "Were they really better than we were?" Were southern players better than northern players? The answer I think is, "Probably not!"

PLAYER AND TEAM EVOLUTION

"Baseball is a team sport played by individuals for themselves."

—Joe Torre

The players from the 1967 Ely Fagan New York State American Legion Baseball Championship team improved our performances as we progressed from Little League to, and through, the college and professional levels of baseball competition. We evolved. We learned the game of baseball, learned to like and love the game of baseball, and we mastered baseball's various aspects of hitting, fielding, throwing, and base running. We mastered what it was we were supposed to do on the baseball field, no matter what the situation. Yes, a couple of the players, Gary Junge and Don Leege, even gave professional baseball a chance, and Gary Junge progressed, pitched, and played pro ball for 6 seasons. Gary was able to progress, and evolve, to the level of pro ball that was just one step below the Major Leagues! This evolution wasn't the result of luck but the result of consistent practice and play over many years. God-given or natural talent to play baseball successfully at high levels of performance, and exceptional eye-hand coordination were part of the players', and ultimately the team's, success for sure. And support from parents, the baseball communities of Rush-Henrietta, East Rochester, and Fairport, numerous volunteers, coaches, and managers also played a vital part in all of it too. But in the end, the players did the work on and off the field, and it was the Ely Fagan players' drive, dedication, and commitment to excellence that made the difference and equipped us to become 1967 New York State champs! We learned how to play together as a team and evolved as a team to the point we knew each other's baseball moves, capabilities, strengths, and weaknesses. Each player recognized what needed to be done in each and every game situation, and each player tried his best to come through with the big hit, the best pitch, or the needed defensive play in order to contribute to the win. The 1967 baseball season was, in some ways, the culmination of—the evolution of—what all the Ely Fagan players had accomplished in our remarkable baseball lives up to that point.

COLLEGES, UNIVERSITIES, AND ADDITIONAL BASEBALL

After our amazing 1967 season and winning the New York State American Legion Championship, Ely Fagan players didn't stop there. We continued on to attend and play baseball at various colleges and universities. Here they are!

Clarkson University
The University of Arizona
Monroe Community College
The University of Rochester
State University of New York at Brockport
The University of Buffalo
Auburn University
Furman University
Ithaca College
Bowling Green University
Bucknell University

And we then had the good fortune to play against many fine baseball teams. Here they are!

Arizona State, Alfred State, University of Maine, Mississippi State, Stetson, North Carolina, South Carolina, Navy, Villanova, Jacksonville State, Cortland State, Eastern Michigan, Kent State, Richmond, Arkansas, Colgate, East Carolina, Florida Southern,

LSU, Purdue, Penn State, Lehigh, The Citadel, Clemson, Pittsburgh, VMI, Cincinnati, Michigan, Northern Illinois, Alabama, Texas A & M, Old Dominion, St. Lawrence, Springfield, South Alabama, Tennessee, Georgia, Vanderbilt, Arizona Western, Prescott College, Chandler College, Northern Arizona University, Cochise College, Grand Canyon College, Georgia Tech, Mississippi, Oneonta State, Hartwick, Fairly Dickinson, Seton Hall, Toledo, Niagara, Radford, St. Bonaventure, Army, Holy Cross, Binghamton, Lafayette, Towson, LaSalle, College of Charleston, Samford, Winthrop, Wofford, Mercer, East Tennessee State, Western Carolina, Appalachian State, Wake Forest, UNC Asheville, St. Joseph's, Youngstown State, Ohio, Dayton, Miami (OH), Western Michigan, Wright State, Ball State, Oakland, Belmont, Central Michigan, Alabama A & M, UCF, UT-Martin, Coastal Carolina, Buffalo, University of Rochester, East Stroudsburg, King's College, Mesa Community College, Mohave Community College, Pima Community College, Glendale Community College, Potsdam, Sienna, Syracuse, Utica, LeMoyne, University of Scranton, Clarkson, SUNY Canton, Elmira, Oswego, RPI, Fredonia, C. W. Post, Salisbury State, William & Mary, Newport News, Florida Southern, Cornell, and Loyola of Baltimore.

So, many of the Ely Fagan players progressed from Little League to Babe Ruth and Senior League, to American Legion Baseball, to Semi-Pro and Muni-League, and in Gary Junge's case—to the prestigious Cape Cod Summer Baseball League—and then we went on to Division I, II, and III levels of college and university baseball. Joe Haefner was an exceptional player and power hitter, and he earned All-American honors while a baseball player at Auburn University. Don Leege set hitting records at Furman University, Al Pannoni was outstanding at the University of Buffalo, yours truly matched or set hitting and fielding records at Ithaca College, Ralph Clapp was a standout at Bowling Green State University, Bob Porta at Bucknell, and Rene Piccarreto was a triple threat and set various hitting, base stealing, and fielding records at the University of Rochester. Bill Kreger and Joe Baldassare excelled at Brockport State. And a couple of Ely Fagan's players earned the opportunity to play in the pro baseball ranks: Don Leege played as a catcher in the San Diego Padres organization, and Gary Junge was an outstanding professional pitcher for over 6 years. He attained the Triple A (AAA) level of competition in the Chicago Cubs organization, and he compiled a very respectable ERA of 3.71.

DUCKS ON THE POND

"Little League Baseball is a very good thing because it keeps the parents off the streets."
— Yogi Berra

All of the 1967 Ely Fagan American Legion players had terrific Little League coaches, including yours truly. I remember hearing my East Rochester Little League coach, Don Leege, Sr., shouting the words "Ducks on the Pond" when there were 2 or 3 baserunners, and I stepped into the batters' box. "Ducks on the Pond, Ducks on the Pond!" He never explained what he meant. For the first several times I heard him shout that, I'd look to the outfield and beyond the fence, searching for ducks and a pond! I'd look and look and look. No ducks, and no pond anywhere! Eventually, I figured he wanted me to get a hit, and drive in some runs. All I know is, when he shouted those words, I heard them as strong words of encouragement. I understood him to be saying to me, "Get a hit!" When I heard those words, I didn't tense up. Instead, I became laser focused and determined to come through for Mr. Leege and the team. I really, really wanted to get a hit, and I didn't want to disappoint. I swear . . . when I heard those words, and the ball was coming into the hitting zone, it seemed to look more like a beach ball than a Little League size baseball!

East Rochester ("ER") is a little town/village in upstate New York, and at the time I was playing Little League, it had a population of around 7,000. Its physical size was around 2 square miles. Although small in size, it has always been big in heart, with the community supporting sports excellence and it is known as the "Home of Champions." Golf course architect Robert Trent Jones once lived in ER, former US Amateur Golf Champion Sam Urzetta grew up in ER, and the 1966 Senior League Baseball World Championship Team hailed from East Rochester. Numerous town, county, and state championship players and teams, coaches and sports officials have come from ER. In short, ER has had a remarkable tradition and history of sports excellence.

Back in the 1950s, the ER Little League Program was exceptional. It was a big deal, and I know it was a big deal because of the coaches, parents, community support, and the numerous volunteers who helped make it and maintain it that way. Back then, baseball became a way of life for many boys and their families. I like to call it the "Golden Age of Little League" because baseball was truly the American Pastime, youth activity, and an essential part of the ER Community.

Little League players looked up to many of the greatest Major League players from that time, and of all time. Mickey Mantle, Yogi Berra, Al Kaline, Willie Mays, Hank Aaron, Ted Williams, Pee Wee Reese, Duke Snider, Eddie Mathews, Whitey Ford, Warren Spahn, Frank Robinson, Brooks Robinson, Jackie Robinson, Minnie Minoso, Roy "Campy" Campanella, Richie Ashburn, and many, many others were revered by so many, their names became household names in many ER homes and throughout the ER community. Boys traded Major League player cards on a daily basis. Mantle for Mays, Spahn for Ford, Snider for Williams, and so on. Many boys clipped baseball cards to the spokes of their bike wheels. "Click, click, click" could be heard as boys rode their bicycles up and down streets and sidewalks all over town. Little did they know the cards in the spokes would someday be worth hundreds, and in some cases, thousands of dollars! Ah, those were the days!

Summers were consumed by baseball. If we weren't playing baseball games, we were practicing baseball. And if we weren't playing or practicing with our teams, we got together, formed our own teams, and played our own games on one of the ER open fields. We set up the field and the bases, and spent additional hours hitting, fielding, throwing, running, and enjoying base-ball—unsupervised—on our own from early morning to early evening . . . when, as darkness set in, we could hear our mothers and fathers calling us to come home!

We usually practiced evenings, after dinner, until dark, several times each week during the summer months of July and August. Practices were structured by coach-brothers, Don and Milt Leege. They stressed fundamentals and situations, and had us respond-ing on the field to practically every game situation we could pos-sibly encounter. Ground ball after ground ball, fly ball after fly ball, drill after drill, situation after situation. By the time games rolled around, we were well-schooled as to what to do, how to do it, why to do it, and where and when to do it.

Responding to those practice situations became second nature during game situations because we had practiced them over and over before, and we were well-prepared, ready, and able to exe-cute. And we were schooled to be alert and focused during prac-tice and games . . . to be tuned in and engaged on every pitch and play . . . to be disciplined, not to daydream or be distracted. We learned to stay involved, immersed in game play and to have or-ganized, appropriate thoughts. We learned to respond positively, we learned how not to panic. No matter what the situation, we learned how to anticipate what could happen before it happened, and how to prepare for the unexpected as though it was expected. Our mental, emotional, and physical preparedness were superior. We didn't feel negative pressure because of our positive, compre-hensive preparedness. That's why we usually won our games, that's why we made very few mistakes, and that's why some of us with outstanding, God-given eye-hand coordination, went on to do well in baseball as we progressed from Little League to Senior League to high school, to college/university baseball, and in some cases, to professional baseball.

Thank you, Don and Milt Leege. Thank you for caring. Thank

you for helping to teach me, and many others, the game of baseball. Thank you for your selflessness, for your sacrifice of time, energy, and for your commitment to excellence. Thank you for believing in all your players. Thank you for the respect and consideration you gave us. Your teaching and coaching helped us learn baseball, and more importantly, helped us to learn about life. The lessons you taught us about baseball and life have served us well. Your teachings and all you shared, continue to live on through us, your former Little League team players.

"Ducks on the pond, ducks on the pond!"

THE GAME OF CATCH

"Defense to me is the key to playing baseball."
—Willie Mays

Some of our grandfathers were part of our sports lives. My grandfather Carl liked sports in general, and he especially loved baseball. He told me he played semi-pro baseball as a catcher in Rochester, New York, and I remember him telling me about the time legendary Yankee Babe Ruth came to town for an exhibition game. I also remember Grandpa having words of praise for Hall of Fame Yankee catcher Bill Dickey. Born in 1904, Grandpa lived and worked through the Depression years, doing odd jobs like selling popcorn on Rochester's street corners, and making a living driving a bus, serving as a chauffeur, and being an independent taxicab driver. Grandpa loved to drive, and he was extremely good at it. His driving record was flawless. No accidents in over 250,000 miles driven! He was truly a courteous, considerate, professional driver.

Grandpa loved to play catch with me. After all, he was a former catcher, and that's what catchers loved to do. He had a rule when we played catch. Neither one of us could wear a mitt. So we always played catch bare-handed, and we always played catch with a hardball. At first, I was apprehensive about this. And at the beginning, it hurt to catch that hardball Grandpa threw to me. He didn't hold back. He zipped the ball to me, and I quickly learned not to let the ball smash into my fingertips, fingers, and hands. Ouch! Yes, at the beginning, and as part of the learning process, I experienced some painful moments, bloodied hands and jammed

fingers, but eventually I learned how to relax—relax my hands—
and I learned how to accept the ball he threw with "soft" hands. I
learned how to welcome the ball into my hands, no matter the velocity, and use my body, arms, and hands in ways that softened
the ball's impact. Grandpa threw hard and easy, he threw the ball
high and low, from one side to the other, over and over. Our game
of catch helped develop my eye-hand coordination and muscle
memory to the extent I eventually mastered the art and science of
catching a baseball.

Those games of catch with Grandpa, after our family dinners
on Sunday afternoons, served me well as I progressed from Little
League through college baseball competition. Thanks, Grandpa!

Grandpa Carl
Circa May 1970, Ithaca College.

THE CANDY KITCHEN

Way back in the 1950s–early 1960s "Golden Days of Little League" when our Little League all-star teams won in tournament play, those victories were celebrated by our local communities. Articles citing those victories appeared in local newspapers, and residents were able to follow their teams' progress. The communities knew the players and their parents, and they were proud of their Little Leaguers' accomplishments.

Our Little League team from East Rochester celebrated victories with special, post-game treats at one of our favorite village restaurants, the Candy Kitchen. Did the players and their parents pay for those treats? No, those special ice cream and fountain drink treats were paid by my grandfather, Carl Bowman. Still in their uniforms, excited players and friends raced back to town, and into the Candy Kitchen after their tournament game wins, to enjoy the best tasting, homemade, and hand-crafted fountain drinks, milkshakes, and ice cream floats money could buy. Grandpa loved doing it, and our players loved those well-earned treats. Ah, those were the days!

*Little Leaguers celebrate victory at the
Candy Kitchen, East Rochester, NY.*

WHERE DID THE CLOTHESPINS GO?

Back in the early 1960s, we had a clothesline strung in our side yard at home, where my mother would use clothespins to fasten our clothes to dry outside in the fresh air. She kept her clothespins in a tattered, cloth clothespin bag which hung from the clothesline. I was happy to help her fasten our wet clothes onto the clothesline and take them down after they were dry when she asked me to help her out. I became curious one day about how one of those clothespins would react when I hit it with my baseball bat. I was pleasantly surprised when I hit that first clothespin because it flew fast and far! So, when I had some extra free time, and when no one was looking, I'd go to my side yard with my bat in hand, and reach into my mother's clothespin bag, and pull out some of those clothespins, toss them up in the air, and hit them with my bat. Our clothespins were solid wood with slits down the middle, and they really traveled high and far when I connected with the solid wooden ends. Over and over, I would hit them and watch them soar high over neighbors' houses or zoom across their backyards. After 5 minutes or so, that full bag of clothespins would dwindle down in number, and I would stop hitting them so we would still have enough left over for our clothes. Fortunately, we seemed to always have spares in the basement, so we could refill the bag after my side yard batting practices! I loved hitting baseballs, whiffle balls, and golf balls out on our expansive high school fields, and yes, I even loved hitting clothespins from time to time in my side yard at home. I knew hitting all those things helped my eye-hand coordination improve, and as a result I became a better hitter of pitched baseballs. How many months or years did I hit clothespins? I only did it occasionally for a summer or 2 because we bought a clothes dryer.

It Came Naturally

If you talk to, and ask, the Ely Fagan players where their talents playing baseball came from, we'd probably say something like, "It was God-given," or "I guess I got it from Mom, or Dad, or my grandparents!" I suppose there's some truth to that. Lots that happens in life can revert back to the age-old nature vs. nurture debate. For instance, it's really not 100 percent certain where outstanding eye-hand coordination comes from, but being born with, and sustaining, keen eyesight might explain some of it. Strength, agility, speed, body size, shape, and weight are other physical factors. Then there are other important factors, such as the ability to focus, confidence, lack of fear, and the determination to succeed. There's the component of being able to instantly, and almost automatically, adjust and adapt effectively to game changing situations as they present themselves. Then there's the ability to anticipate those game situations before they even occur, so that if and when they do present themselves, the response is quick, forceful, and spot on. Attentiveness and awareness also come into play.

Then there's player temperament. Is the player a "hothead"? Is the player able to effectively deal with frustration, control anger, muster and channel adrenaline effectively, turn it on and off as game situations require? Is the player able to block out crowd noise and other distractions? You can readily see these, and many other factors, go into determining player talent and success. And of course, let's not overlook the ever-important component of baseball practice, including hitting practice, throwing and catching practice, base running practice, on-the-field game knowledge, and situation practice.

I think there are a couple of other factors. They are the player motivation, and the player and baseball environment. How motivated is the player? What kind of baseball environment did the player find himself in? Did the motivating factors come from within the player, outside the player, or were they a combination of both? Did the player strive for success? Did the player encounter a favorable, supportive baseball-playing environment (with adequate equipment, field, instruction, family and community support, positive coaching, etc.) or not? How effective was the player at overcoming hardship? So much and more determines player talent and success.

In the end, though, Ely Fagan players as a group would say, "It came naturally!" Yes, we practiced and played, but after a while, what we did on the baseball field—having done it so many times before, over and over—became natural for us. Yes, it came naturally!

KNOW AND PROTECT THE STRIKE ZONE

Hitters don't like to be called out on strikes. Good hitters know the strike zone, they know when to swing at pitches, and when not to swing at pitches. Coaches have often told hitters, "A walk is as good as a hit" mainly because coaches don't like seeing their hitters swinging wildly at pitches that are way outside the strike zone. But when hitters have 2 strikes on them, it makes sense to protect the plate by swinging at pitches that are "close" to being called strikes instead of taking those pitches and being called out by home plate umpires.

Umpires know the strike zone and for the most part do a consistent and accurate job of calling balls and strikes. Do they ever make mistakes? Yes, they do. Sometimes umpires make mistakes, but when they do, players usually accept their calls, move on, and don't complain or whine. The Major Leagues have instant replay and review to check close and controversial umpire field calls, and when proven wrong, field umpires reverse calls to make it right. Umpires know the rules of the game of baseball, and they enforce those rules best they can. In a way, umpires could be viewed as on-field "judges" and "police" because they do their best to make sure players and coaches don't cheat and always follow the rules of the game. And when players and coaches get way out of line, umpires can, and sometimes do, eject them from the playing field. Umpires try their best to maintain proper player, and coach, conduct and behavior during games, and they do their best to assure the rules of the game are followed.

The game of baseball, its rules, and umpire game management and control help teach players, coaches, and fans how to win honestly, lose graciously, and practice good sportsmanship. I think those of us who have played the game of baseball, and have learned and practiced those important principles, become better equipped to grow up having a healthy respect for authority, rules, and regulations. Furthermore, I think former players also stand a pretty good chance of becoming law abiding and productive citizens. Add it all up, and former baseball players just might be better prepared to navigate life's uncertainties, trials, and tribulations partly because they've learned how to swing at strikes and "protect the strike zone."

"Take Me Out, Coach!"

The Ely Fagan baseball players wanted to win and we never gave up. That positive, winning attitude was a critical component of our success. When the players took the field, it was with conviction and determination. Players wanted to give our all for the entire game, and we weren't satisfied unless we gave our best effort, and that effort resulted in a team win. When Gary Junge, or Joe Baldassare or Andy Haefner or John Kokinda or any other Ely Fagan pitchers took the mound, it was with their all-out effort, belief, and determination. Coach Petersen believed in his pitchers, and the pitchers knew the coach was watching, supporting, and encouraging them and their pitching efforts. They knew Coach Petersen believed in them.

When I coached high school baseball many years ago, I once inherited a group of players who lacked confidence and baseball skills, but I did my best to teach, support, and encourage them, and I hoped, over time, they would eventually learn to believe in themselves as they improved. Sure enough, some of the players evolved, and became better baseball players, and it was gratifying to see them start believing in themselves.

One of the pitchers was pretty good, he had a nice fastball and decent control, but he lacked toughness and determination, and when the going got tough, he decided he wanted to get going! He wanted me to take him out of games he pitched in when he got nervous, or when he was challenged by hitters, or when he thought he'd pitched enough. I'd walk out to the mound to talk to him during a game to see how he was feeling, to find out what he

71

was thinking, and he'd look at me and say, "Please take me out, Coach!" His fastball and control were fine, but when he decided he'd had enough, he'd ask me to take him out! So, I concluded this was a teachable moment, and I decided he needed to figure out how to get through and over his mental, emotional, and confidence "meltdowns," so I refused to take him out of the game. He failed to overcome his demons a few times, but he eventually learned how to manage himself, and get through and over those tough patches, and from then on, he was able to handle his pitching fears. He developed into a consistent, winning pitcher. Once he figured it out for himself, he replaced the "Take me out, Coach," with "Leave me in, Coach!"

MUSCLE MEMORY

Baseball—like most sports—rewards practice and repetition of movement, and development of muscle memory. Throwing, catching, hitting, running the bases over and over in purposeful, errorless, flawless ways sends messages to and from the mind and body that "I know what to do, I know how to do it, and I can and will do it!" Development of muscle memory results in increased confidence because flawless and purposeful repetition results in success, and the future and further success becomes an extension of prior and current success. From Little League, when fundamentals are learned, practiced, and played, to and through high school, American Legion Baseball, college baseball, and beyond, players evolve and develop their mental and physical skills and abilities to the point where playing becomes almost automatic. Player actions and reactions to baseball game situations are welcomed, anticipated, and responded to with power and precision, elegance and grace. Over time, players develop extraordinary muscle memory, and situational game mistakes are seldom made.

THE PLAYER INSIDE

"Baseball is like church.
Many attend. Few understand."
—Leo Durocher

    Spectators love watching athletic events, no matter the game, and they look for special things to happen on the athletic field. Baseball has always been one of the most popular spectator sports. Since baseball's inception, fans have been sitting in their stadium seats, or standing near the playing field to get a closer look at players hitting, fielding, running, sliding, and throwing the baseball. Fans know the game of baseball provides its share of unique sights, sounds, and special memories. There's the "crack of the bat," when the hitter solidly connects with a pitcher's fastball. There's the unmistakable sound generated by a pitcher's fastball hitting the pocket of the catcher's mitt. There's the sound of the baseball hitting the leather of the infielder's glove, and the first baseman's glove when the infielder throws the ball over to him. There's the occasional umpire dispute when a player or coach disagrees with an umpire's decision, and that can be exciting, and even entertaining, to see. In a 9-inning baseball game, lots can happen for sure, and fans can find themselves being part of baseball history. They could witness a no-hitter, or even an extremely rare perfect game. Whether watching a Little League game, or a college, professional, or even Major League game, spectators could see some amazing plays, and because of that, spectators show up at baseball games time and time again, year after year.

Spectators have an outer view of all the action. The action speaks for itself, it is honest and on full display for spectators to see. It's real, and in plain sight, but there's another perspective of what's happening on the baseball field, and that's the players' "inner perspective" and the decisions players make. The decisions baseball players make in the heat of competition can be proactive, reactive, or even a combination of both. Those decisions are a combination of physical, mental, and emotional baseball intelligence, and those decisions are oftentimes made in split seconds. Spectators who were, or are also, baseball players can sometimes relate to what they see because they've been there and done something similar on the baseball field. Experienced, well-prepared baseball players know the game is largely a game of anticipation. Players have learned what to do in various situations, and anticipate whatever comes their way before it happens, and know in their minds what they'll do in response to situations they'll be faced with. There's truth in the old adage "practice makes perfect" when it comes to playing baseball. Even today, the remaining Ely Fagan players attest to that as they reflect back on their super 1967 season. Back in 1967, the spectators who watched Ely Fagan's legion games gained a lasting appreciation for all they did. Those spectators who paid attention back then learned to appreciate "The Player Inside."

Broken Bats and Baseballs

"Back in my day, we didn't think about money as much. We enjoyed playing the game. We loved baseball. I didn't think about anybody else but the Cardinals."
—**Stan Musial**

In the 1950s, when we played baseball between our ages of 5 and 10, we used old-fashioned wooden bats and relatively inexpensive baseballs. I think back then, a youth size and weight wooden baseball bat cost several dollars, and baseballs could be had for around $1.00. Back then, a gallon of gasoline cost around $0.25! At my town barbershop, I could buy a small-sized, ice-cold bottle of Coca-Cola for a dime. Wooden clarinet reeds cost $0.25. Baseball mitts cost between $10.00 and $20.00. A movie ticket for a double-feature Saturday matinee, 20 cartoons, and gift and toy giveaways cost $0.40! A hamburger at our local "Burger Park" cost $0.25, and a bag of French fries cost $0.10.

Over time, our bats cracked and the covers on our baseballs started to loosen, and even come apart at the seams. That didn't stop us. Yes, maybe our play was interrupted, but we discovered remedies to fix our cracked bats and baseballs. No, it didn't enter our minds we needed new equipment, at least not at first. First, we thought about what we needed to repair what was wrong so we could start playing again.

We turned to nails and screws to "heal" the cracks in our bats. Then, after pounding in the nails or tightening the screws, we'd tightly wrap the damaged sections of the bat handle with some sticky, black tape. Round and round we'd wrap the tape around the bat handle and cracked area, covering the repaired areas nicely, and making the bat handle and bat solid again. Ah, after that we'd usually be ready to "play ball," and our bats would be ready to hit baseballs again! Same with our scarred and coverless baseballs. Wrap them with tape, and we'd be ready to go! It didn't matter to us whether our bats and baseballs were new or old. We were happy just to be able to play the game!

It Wasn't Just
about Baseball

"The ballplayer who loses his head, who can't keep his cool, is worse than no ballplayer at all."
—**Lou Gehrig**

Back in the 1950s, and during our summer school break, we would leave the house early most mornings, get on our bikes, and ride to the baseball field where we would play all day long. We didn't even eat lunch. Yes, we would drink water, but the fun of being together with friends, and playing baseball on a sunny day under a bright, blue sky was most important to us. We got lost in our play, hitting and fielding, catching and throwing, running the bases. Games would be won and lost, plays would sometimes be argued or disputed, "I was safe!" "You were out!" "Safe!" "Out!" And in the end, we'd figure it out. Disputes would be handled, even if one player or team didn't agree with the decision. We settled it and moved on. When we moved on to another play, another inning, another game, the past was left behind. Old disputes were forgotten. We learned how to get along.

It really didn't always matter who was right or wrong. What mattered most was we were having a good time, and arguing slowed the good time down, and arguing past a certain point became a waste of time. None of us wanted to waste our time because we knew, moving ahead, there would be many more good times to experience together. We had so much fun, in fact, we'd lose track of the time. But when the sun went down, and it got much darker, and we found we had a hard time seeing the baseball, we knew the day was almost done and we'd need to return home on our bikes. We'd force our eyes to adjust and play as long as possible into the darkness. We clung to every minute we had out there on our baseball field.

Yes, all that playing and practicing helped to make us better at playing baseball. It was good, clean fun, and being outside most days in the fresh air and sunshine didn't hurt. But maybe more importantly, we learned how to get along. We learned how to negotiate. We learned that sometimes we won, and other times we lost, but whatever happened, we learned how to handle being winners or losers, and how to be good sports, no matter what happened. We learned how not to whine. We learned how not to bicker. We learned how not to cheat. We learned how to make friends and keep friends. We learned how to share, how to be supportive, and we learned how to control our anger and frustration. We learned how to be independent. We learned about self-reliance. We developed confidence. We learned to be tolerant of others, and we learned the meaning of respect.

Yes, we learned a lot about baseball way back in the 1950s, but more importantly, we also learned many valuable life lessons. We ultimately learned what we were doing wasn't just about playing the game of baseball. We learned what we were doing was about life itself.

DIRT IN YOUR
SHOES AND SOCKS!

During summers, way back in the 1950s, when we were young kids growing up in East Rochester and learning the game of baseball, we would make our own fun. We'd lay out the bases, fences, home plate, and the pitcher's mound, then we'd choose teams, and play from 9 in the morning until darkness and dinner time. It was glorious, unsupervised fun, and we hated to see the daylight fade as the sun began to set behind the tall hill at Harris Field. At about that time in the late afternoon, we'd hear our mothers shout to us to come home! We'd ignore those first calls to come home and keep playing, but after the second or third time, we knew our mothers meant business, and we'd better stop playing. So we'd stop playing, hop on our bikes, and peddle home fast. When we arrived home, Mom would be standing at the kitchen door with her hands on her hips. Then we'd hear the words, "Take off your shoes and socks before you come in!" So, we'd sit down on the steps and take them off, and dirt would go everywhere. Then she'd say, "You brought half the field back home with you in those shoes and socks!" She was right. We were sweaty, dirty, and there was dirt everywhere. So, we'd march up to take a quick bath and clean up before eating dinner. Yes, our moms were glad to see us when we returned home from Harris Field, and they could tell we had played our hardest, they could tell we had played on our own, and they were happy for us even though we, and our shoes and socks, were covered with dirt! Even though we were filthy dirty our moms knew we had been out in fresh air and sunshine having good, clean fun!

THE LITTLE LEAGUE BANQUETS

At the conclusion of our Rochester-area Little League seasons, players, coaches, and families were invited to their post-season Little League banquets. Everyone looked forward to attending the annual banquets. The festivities and dinners were great, and regular season and playoff winners were awarded trophies. The banquets started in the early evening, everyone arrived in their "Sunday Best," and found their teammates, coaches, and their designated tables. Delicious meals were served, and after that the awards ceremony took place, and then the guest speakers addressed the audience from their head table location. The food was always very tasty, and the guest speakers were always accomplished baseball players or coaches.

The Rochester Red Wings players and coaches were frequent guest speakers, and they always provided inspiration and encouragement. And they, along with other Rochester-area baseball celebrities, took time to meet players and sign autographs. It was great fun, and the Little Leaguers loved it. Johnny Antonelli, Billy DeMars, and Joe Altobelli were guest speakers during my Little League days.

The Rochester baseball community, including the Rochester Red Wings organization, was always accessible and supportive of their area's Little League programs and players. They wanted to make a difference, and they did make a meaningful and lasting difference year after year.

Little League Banquet Lists John Antonelli

Approximately 300 Little Leaguers and their parents will gather for the final time this year at the Country House Wednesday night for the annual awards banquet.

East Rochester Junior Baseball Assn. president Peter Quinzi announced that major league pitcher Johnny Antonelli and several other top baseball personalities will be present.

Antonelli is a former American Legion pitching wizard who was beaten in a game at Eyer Park by East Rochester's Fish Post team in a memorable game 15 years ago.

Other speakers will be Ed Bastian of the Rochester Red Wing office staff, and Billy De-Mars, a former Buffalo and ex-major leaguer.

Jim Pannucci, District 5 director of Little League, will present awards to members of the ER All Stars, who came within two victories of copping the New York State title last August. The

All Stars number 17 players collected from the six team circuit.

Awards also are slated for the members of Don and Milt Leege's Tiger team, which won the regular season championship, and the playoff champs, Pat Piscini and Jacques Brothers' Hornets.

OCT 1961

OCT 1963

Coach Leege and Lou Baldassare

VISUALIZATION

*"Baseball is 90 percent mental and
the other half is physical."*
—Yogi Berra

During baseball season, and especially on nights before games, Ely Fagan players would prepare mentally for the next day's game. Pitchers would think about pitch locations, pitch speed, pitches to use, and so on. Hitters would think about, and visualize, pitched balls coming into the home plate area. Hitters would visualize pitched balls coming into the hitting area that were fast balls, breaking balls, balls thrown to the outside of the plate, inside of the plate, balls thrown high and low, and then process how they would react to those pitches. Batters would visualize the ball and the swing they would make to connect with the ball . . . no matter where the pitch ended up in the strike zone.

Each anticipated situation would be visualized, processed, and prepared for in advance of the next day's game. The mental preparation and visualization were crucial components in getting ready for games, and having success in games. Additionally, players prepared mentally and visually for various fielding situations and plays. Visualization, at home, of catching fly balls, ground balls, and thrown balls helped make it happen successfully on the field in the next day's game.

Physical "on-the-field" preparations, drills, and actual, repetitive hitting, throwing, catching, fielding, and base running were fundamental to eye-hand and physical coordination and success for sure. The "off the field" mental and visual preparation of how it should all happen contributed significantly to player and team success, and doing all the right things in the next day's game.

GETTING THERE

Each of the 1967 Ely Fagan team players had already spent years and years practicing and playing baseball by the time we walked onto the field at the beginning of that special, championship summer season. Each player had begun his journey in baseball in the early to mid-1950s—a golden age in baseball—with enthusiastic local community support, family support, and Little League fields springing up all across America. Little League Baseball became a constant for the Ely Fagan players in each of the Rochester, New York communities. And when we weren't playing Little League, and as time allowed, players also practiced and played on our own on fields around town.

We rode our bikes to and from our homes to our fields of play, often with baseball cards pinned to our bike spokes. We heard the "click, click, click" repetitive sounds the pinned cards made as we peddled down the roads and sidewalks to our destinations. Yes, those were the days, and in today's collector's market, those old "click, click, click" cards that were pinned to the bike spokes, and ended up tattered, torn, scraped, and bent would be worth thousands and thousands of dollars!

After Little League Baseball came the Babe Ruth League, or Senior League Baseball, and high school baseball and then, with improved talent and baseball knowledge, skills, overall ability, motivation, and continued interest and commitment, American Legion Baseball in the summertime.

By the time Ely Fagan players reached the American Legion level, many had part-time or full-time, summer day jobs. So, from

Monday to Friday, players practiced or played evening games, and we played day games on Saturdays and Sundays. The love of baseball kept us going all summer long, as did the love of winning, because winning and success prevailed from start to finish.

What was behind Ely Fagan's winning and success? It should come as no surprise that dominant pitching, hitting, fielding, and base running were the main reasons, along with an amazing coach, Harold Petersen, and the ongoing parent and community support.

The 1967 Ely Fagan New York State American Legion Baseball Team Championship Season

1. Monday, 6/26/67—Wm. W. Doud vs. Ely Fagan at Gates-Chili HS WON
2. Wednesday, 6/28/67—Ely Fagan vs. Fishbaugh at Rush-Henrietta HS WON
3. Friday, 6/30/67—Goodridge vs. Ely Fagan at Spencerport HS WON
4. Monday, 7/3/67—Ely Fagan vs. Miller at Rush-Henrietta HS WON
5. Wednesday, 7/5/67—Fish vs. Ely Fagan at Eyer Park WON
6. Friday, 7/7/67—Ely Fagan vs. Irondequoit at Rush-Henrietta HS WON
7. Monday, 7/10/67—Ely Fagan vs. Warner at Rush-Henrietta HS WON
8. Wednesday, 7/12/67—Greece vs. Ely Fagan at Mooney HS WON
9. Friday, 7/14/67—Ely Fagan vs. Noone at Rush-Henrietta WON
10. Monday, 7/17/67—Magill vs. Ely Fagan at Charlotte WON

11. Wednesday, 7/19/67—Ely Fagan vs. Seaman at Rush-Henrietta WON

12. Monday, 7/24/67—Veterans vs. Ely Fagan at Aquinas HS WON

13. Wednesday, 7/26/67—Ely Fagan vs. Braman at Rush-Henrietta HS WON

14. Friday, 7/28/67—Ely Fagan vs. Doud at Rush-Henrietta HS WON

15. Saturday, 7/29/67—7th District Championship Play Offs, Ely Fagan defeated Sodus 3–2 at Colburn Park, Newark, New York, Winning Pitcher Gary Junge—15 strikeouts WON

16. Monday, 7/31/67—Fishbaugh vs. Ely Fagan at Hilton HS WON

17. Tuesday, 8/1/67—7th District Semi-Final Game, Ely Fagan defeated East Bloomfield 5–0 at Coburn Park, Newark, New York, Winning Pitcher Gary Junge—allowed 2 Hits WON

18. Wednesday, 8/2/67—Ely Fagan vs. Goodridge at Rush-Henrietta HS WON

19. Friday, 8/4/67—Miller vs. Ely Fagan at Pittsford HS—WON

20. Saturday, 8/5/67—7th District Championship Game, Ely Fagan defeated Corning 5–1 at Bath, New York, Winning Pitcher Gary Junge WON

21. Monday, 8/7/67—Ely Fagan vs. Fish at Rush-Henrietta HS WON

22. Wednesday, 8/9/67—Irondequoit vs. Ely Fagan at Kearney HS WON

23. Friday, 8/11/67—Warner vs. Ely Fagan at Webster HS LOST

24. Saturday, 8/12/67—Section D Championship Game, 7th District Champions vs. 8th District Champions, Ely Fagan defeated Troop 1 Post of Buffalo at Batavia, NY, Winning Pitcher Gary Junge WON

25. Monday, 8/14/67—Ely Fagan vs. Greece at Rush-Henrietta HS WON

26. Tuesday, 8/15/67—New York State Semi-Final Championship Game, Ely Fagan defeated Andrean Post Utica at Sharon Park, Geneva, New York 8–6, Winning Pitcher Gary Junge WON

27. Wednesday, 8/16/67—Noone vs. Ely Fagan at Churchville HS WON

28. Saturday, 8/19/67—New York State American Legion Championship Game, Ely Fagan defeated Tappan Post Staten Island at Doubleday Field, Cooperstown, New York, 1–0 in 13 innings, Winning Pitcher Andy Haefner in relief, Gary Junge pitched 12 innings, and had 13 strikeouts, and gave up 3 hits and WON!!

ELY FAGAN BECOMES FIRST AND ONLY ROCHESTER-AREA TEAM TO EVER CAPTURE THE NY STATE AMERICAN LEGION CHAMPIONSHIP!

Legion State Baseball Final Here Saturday

Defending champion A d r e a n Post of Utica was scheduled to meet Ely Fagan Post of Henrietta at Syracuse, and Tappan Post 125 of Staten Island was to play Plattsburgh at Schenectady Tuesday afternoon in the semi-finals of the annual New York State American Legion baseball tournament.

The state tournament final will be played at Doubleday Field here on Saturday afternoon at 2 o'clock.

A pair of shutouts featured the quarter-finals. S a t u r d a y with Plattsburgh Post winning a thriller 1-0, on their only hit of the game, a two-out homer in the seventh by Tom Herlihy, center fielder, to defeat Green Island's left-handed Jackie LeMary at Ticonderoga.

In MacArthur Stadium, Batavia, Gary Junge pitched a two-hit, 1-0 victory over Troop I Post, Buffalo, to give Henrietta a berth in the semi-finals. Ely Fagan is now 23 and 1 for the season.

Adrean Post kept in the running with a 7-3 victory over Endicott Post 82 in a game at Oneonta, by virtue of a four-run fifth and three more tallies in the sixth. Ronald Barr pitched a one-hitter for the Uticans.

In Staten Island, Tappan Post 125 took the metropolitan-lower Hudson Valley crown with a 2-1 conquest of Van Cott Post, Nassau County, as John Donovan shaded Ken Beebe in a tight duel.

Clark F. Simmons Post, No. 579, of this village will be official host for the state final with Gerald E. Clark in charge of local arrangements. The game itself will be in charge of Dick Conners, president of the Albany City Council and state chairman of American Legion baseball.

The players will stay at the Mohican Motel here and at the Brookside Motel near Milford. They will be served their meals at the Veterans Club by members of the local Legion post, under the direction of Joseph M. Clancy of the Doubleday Restaurant catering service.

A tour of the National Baseball Hall of Fame is being scheduled for the boys during their stay here.

The annual tournament steak dinner will be served at the Veterans Club Saturday night at which trophies will be formally presented.

The teams will leave for home Sunday morning.

Cooperstown, Otsego County, N. Y., 13326, Wednesday, August 16, 1967

Ely Fagan Nine Snares
State Legion Championship

BRILLIANT — Gary Junge of Ely Fagan Post threw 12 scoreless innings in his team's 13-inning 1-0 win over Tappen Post of Staten Island for the New York State American Legion baseball championship.

Special to The Democrat and Chronicle

COOPERSTOWN — Gary Junge and Joe Baldassare paced Ely Fagan of Rochester to the New York State American Legion baseball crown yesterday. Fagan outlasted Tappen Post of Staten Island, 1-0, in 13 innings at Doubleday Field.

Baldassare's bases-loaded single in the 13th gave Fagan its winning margin in the pitchers' duel. Junge and Tappen hurler John Donovan pitched scoreless ball for 12 innings, the maximum number a pitcher can work under the rules. Junge fanned 13 batters, as did Donovan.

Andy Haefner took the mound in the 13th for Fagan and retired the side in short order. Bob Porta worked Tappen's Gene Guerriero for a walk and Rene Pecarretto doubled, sending him to third.

One out later, Dick Goodwin was intentionally walked to load the bases. Baldassare then ripped a sharp single, sending Porta across the plate with the game's only run.

The victory marks the first time in 16 years that a Rochester American Legion team has successfully progressed farther than regional Legion tournies. Fagan will journey to Bordentown, N.J., Wednesday to play Bordentown, the New Jersey state champs in the opening round of the national tournament.

HE DIDN'T MAKE IT — Pete Wyse of Staten Island gives a valiant try but was out at first base after grounding to infield in championship game of the New York State American Legion Tournament at Cooperstown. Dick Goodwin of Ely Fagan Post, Henrietta, handles the throw. Ely Fagan won in 13 innings. (AP)

Fagan to Battle Today
For State Legion Title

COOPERSTOWN — Ely Fagan Post, the top team in the Monroe County American Legion Baseball League, will meet Tappan Post of Staten Island here at 2 p.m. today for the American Legion State Championship.

Fagan, now 25-1 for the season, won the regional title last week. Tappan Post boasts a 13-1 season tally.

Gary Junge, a 19-year-old with a phenomenal arm, will be on the mound for Fagan. He carries a perfect 11-0 record and has pitched several shutouts this season.

Today's victor will play Bordentown, N.J., in Bordentown on Aug. 23 in the opening round of the national tournament.

THE GAME

"I became a good pitcher when I stopped trying to make them miss the ball, and started trying to make them hit it."
—Sandy Koufax

It was Saturday, August 19, 1967. The stage was set in Cooperstown for the showdown between the 2 best American Legion Baseball teams in New York State. The Tappen Post team from Staten Island and its ace pitcher, Jack Donovan, were eager and ready to play. The Rochester-area Ely Fagan team, and our incomparable hurler, Gary Junge, were rested and excited to play on historic Doubleday Field for the New York State Championship. The weather was hot and sunny, and hundreds of team supporters, friends, relatives, and Cooperstown community baseball enthusiasts flocked in through the main gate as soon as it opened to the public.

The Ely Fagan supporters settled into seats behind home plate and the first base side, and the Tappen Post folks sought the third base seating area, located directly behind their team dugout. Players warmed up on the field, and one could hear the sounds and echoes of bats hitting balls, and balls hitting mitts. Proud parents and grandparents watched intently and expected the game would be evenly matched and a good one.

No one could predict the outcome of this game with total certainty. One thing for sure though, Donovan and Junge were the main reasons for their teams' success. They were both unbeatable. They were unstoppable. They were capable of mowing down hitter after hitter, and the fans knew it. Baseball scouts also knew it. Pro team scouts knew about them and their talents, and stood ready to make them an offer at the appropriate, future time. Fans knew they were most likely in store for a pitchers' duel. What they didn't know was this pitchers' duel between Donovan and Junge would be monumental. It would be historic. Fans didn't know THIS championship game would be a game for the ages.

The game began, and both pitchers effectively settled into their natural rhythms. Both had their normal pinpoint control, and both kept hitters off balance. Neither team mounted an offensive charge because both pitchers struck out one hitter after another as the game progressed from one inning to another. 8 innings, 9 innings, 10 innings, 11 innings, 12 innings passed, and still there was no score! Both Donovan and Junge were still on the mound through 12 innings but then, because of American Legion rules, they were required to leave the game, and couldn't come back to pitch in the 13th inning. In total, for those 12 innings pitched, both Donovan and Junge each struck out 13 batters! Donovan gave up 6 hits and in contrast, the miserly Junge gave up a measly 3 hits. Both Donovan and Junge were given a much-deserved standing ovation. So, in the top of the 13th inning, fire baller Andy Haefner, came into the game for Junge. Haefner was both tall and strong, and he was "fired up" and focused as he took the mound. He was all business, and his tank of adrenaline was full, he was ready to go! "Strike 1!" "Strike 2!" "Strike 3!" The first batter Haefner faced was out on strikes. And then the second batter Haefner faced went down on 3 consecutive strikes. Then, Haefner struck out the third and final batter he faced on 3 pitches! Andy Haefner had just come in to pitch in the most pressure-packed, important game of his life, and the most important game played by the Ely Fagan team, and he struck out the other side . . . all 3 hitters he faced . . . on 9 consecutive pitches! The Ely Fagan players and game spectators went wild with excitement! Suddenly it seemed like the Rochester team had established some new and exciting momentum going into the bottom of the 13th inning. In the bottom of the 13th inning, the Staten Island and Tappen Post relief pitcher, Gene Guerriero, came in for Donovan to face the Ely Fagan hitters. He walked the first batter he faced, Bobby Porta. Then, power hitter Rene Piccarreto smashed a long double to right-center field, moving Porta all the way to third base. Guerriero then retired catcher Richie Petersen. With one out and 2 runners in scoring position, the Tappen Post manager, catcher, and Guerriero decided to walk me. I had already garnered 3 hits in the game against Donovan, so I was intentionally passed to load the bases. That strategy was short-lived, however. The Tappen Post outfielders were playing in close to the infield area, hoping they could prevent the winning run from scoring on a ball hit to them in the outfield. With the outfielders playing shallow, the next hitter, outfielder Joe Baldassare, drove a hard-hit fly ball (which proved to be the game-winning hit) well over the right fielder's head, scoring Porta from third base with the winning run. The Ely Fagan celebration began immediately after Porta crossed home plate. The press/media, family, friends, and the Cooperstown fans took pictures of players, the team manager, dignitaries, and team coach Harold Petersen. Some of the Ely Fagan players were even asked for their autographs! It was a great victory shared by all, and deservedly mostly credited to game heroes Gary Junge, Andy Haefner, and Joe Baldassare. The entire team contributed to the victory of course . . . even the batboys and team scorekeeper had a hand in the team effort . . . but in the end, the win mostly belonged to the brilliant pitching of starting pitcher Gary Junge, the dominant, overpowering, relief pitching of Andy Haefner, the flawless catching by Richie Petersen, a key hit—a double—by Rene Piccarreto, and the clutch game-winning hit by Joe Baldassare. The trip back to Rochester and Rush-Henrietta was a happy one. It was a trip the entire team enjoyed. The players, Coach Peterson, and manager Art Flatt were greeted by an enthusiastic Rochester and Rush-Henrietta community, and celebration, upon our return. It was a time all involved could savor our historic game victory. No other American Legion team from the Rochester area had ever won the New York State American Legion Baseball Championship before the 1967 team. And some years later, it's been reported that local Cooperstown baseball fans, who were at the game, remembered it as the greatest pitchers' duel, and baseball game they had ever seen!

Doubleday Field Front Entrance Views 8/19/1967
Circa June 1989

*Post-game awards ceremony on Doubleday Field. 8/19/1967
American Legion dignitaries along with Ely Fagan team
representatives shown in uniform. Left to Right in uniform: Art
Flatt–Team manager, Ralph Clapp and Rich Goodwin–Co-
Captains, and Harold Petersen–Team Coach.*

Post-Game, on-field celebration 8/19/1967

Coach Petersen,
Ralph Clapp, Al Pannoni

Lou Baldassare, Don Leege
(#18), Gary Junge

Al Pannoni

A very happy Coach Petersen

Joe Baldassare, Gary Junge,
Grandpa Carl Bowman

Joe Haefner, John Kokinda

Andy Haefner, Bill Kreger, Don
Leege, John Kokinda

Rich Petersen

Where there is a sport being played, there you'll find someone from East Rochester, or so it seems. Last Saturday my husband and I, journeyed to Cooperstown, N.Y., to watch the Ely Fagan American

* * *

Legion baseball team compete for the state title. Though this is a Henrietta baseball team, five "bombers" are represented. They were Don Leege, Billy Kreger, Joe Baldassare, Dick Goodwin and John Kokinda.

For baseball lovers, this was a game to be lived through 12 and a half innings of scoreless ball! By that time both pitchers had used up their availability and new men took to the mound.

Ely Fagan's Haepner fanned three-in-a-row in the top of the 13th inning. But the Staten Island pitcher walked the first man, and a supposed sacrifice bunt turned out a hit, so two men were on base.

The next batter struck out and Dick Goodwin received an intentional walk to load the bases. Joe Baldassare, hero of the day, smashed a hit to right field to end the game.

Besides the families of the players, the game was watched by Assemblyman Don Cook, Henrietta, and Assemblyman Charles Stockmeister. Other guests were: Scouts from the San Francisco Giants, L.A. Dodgers, N.Y. Yankees, Baltimore Orioles, Detroit Tigers

Most eyes were on Gary Junge, including those of his aunt and uncle, Mr. and Mrs. Thomas Wagner, E. Elm St. Still in the world of sports. . Westbury, L.I., who won the recent tournament in East Rochester's Regional Senior League recently, went all the way in DesMoines, Iowa, and captured the 1967 World Series crowd.

The game was broadcast to Westbury and over six thousand people stood in the streets to listen to the game over loudspeakers. The team deserved the win, and our congratulations and best wishes go to them.

Rich Goodwin

1967 Ely Fagan team

NEW YORK STATE CHAMPS: Ely Fagan Post baseball team members took time out for this picture enroute to their winning the New York State American Legion Baseball Championship.Standing, from left to right, Commander John Hetrick,scorekeeper Barb Petersen, coach Harold Petersen, Bill Kreger, John Kokinda, Andy Haefner, Gary Junge, Joe Baldassare, Jose Haefner, Rene Piccarreto, Art Flatt, manager, and State Assemblyman Don Cook. Kneeling, from left to right, Dick Goodwin, Rich Petersen, Don Leege, Ralph Clapp, Fred Pannoni, Bob Porta and Harold Andrews, 7th District American Legion chairman. Front row,left to right, batboys Tom Pannoni, Chuck Glaza, holding the New York State championship plaque, and Al Goodwin.

State Champs: Ely Fagan Post

Henrietta's Ely-Fagan Post is in Bordentown, N.J. this week seeking to add to its laurels as New York State American Legion Baseball champions.

Several East Rochester players are members of the championship team. They are: Joe Baldassare, Dick Goodwin, Don Leege, Billy Kreger, and John Kokinda.

The Ely-Fagan team went 13 exciting innings in beating Staten Island's Tappen Post, 1-0, last Saturday at Cooperstown.

Starting hurler Gary Junge went the maximum 12-innings allowed by Legion rules before exiting in a 0-0 ballgame. His sterling performance was spiced with 13 strikeouts and he allowed only three hits over the long route. He walked three, one intentionally.

Andy Haefner took over in the top of the 13th and promptly struck out the side.

In the bottom half of the 13th, second-baseman Bob Porta drew a walk and advanced to third on Rene Piccarreto's double. First baseman Dick Goodwin was walked intentionally, loading

the bases.

Joe Baldassare drove Tappen's Gene Guerriero's first pitch into right field, scoring Porta and sending the happy Henrietta squad home with the victory.

The team was met at the Thruway exit in Victor by members of the Post along with city and county officials who escorted the jubilant victors to Memorial Park where they were honored at the Post's annual picnic.

Six teams will be taking part in the Regional test in New Jersey. The winner of the double elimination tourney will go to Memphis, Tenn. to play in the National American Legion tournament.

Ely-Fagan started on its way to championship with a win over Sodus at Newark. They then moved past East Bloomfield, Corning, Buffalo and Geneva, before winning

the championship at Cooperstown against Staten Island.

Members of the team are shortstop Bill Kreger, Pitcher John Kokinda, pitcher and outfielder Andy Haefner, pitcher Gary Junge, left-fielder and pitcher Joe Baldassare, Cen-

ter-fielder Joe Haefner, rightfielder Rene Piccarreto, first baseman Dick Goodwin,catcher Rich Petersen, utility infielder Don Leege, third baseman Ralph Clapp, shortstop Fred Pannoni and second baseman Bob Porta.

Hail To The Champs

The Autograph

First obtaining and then collecting baseball player autographs has been a time-honored tradition for fans of baseball ever since the very first baseball players took the field. Meeting the player, being near the player, and then obtaining the player's autograph is a special thrill, especially for younger fans. Imagine the thrill of having met, let's say, Hank Aaron or Mickey Mantle or Willie Mays, and then watching Hank, Mickey, or Willie autograph your baseball or piece of paper! Wow! And over the years, and into modern times, that same tradition holds true today. As long as there's baseball, there will be baseball fans, and autographs will always be a fan's cherished keepsake.

After winning the state championship in Cooperstown on Doubleday Field in 1967, some of the younger fans in attendance that August day asked several of the Ely Fagan players for our autographs! These fans had pens in hand and their game programs ready for the players to sign. We players were surprised when the fans asked us for our autographs, but were pleased and honored to oblige! The autographs players gave that day were free of charge. What the players received in return for giving our autographs was something very special. It was the look of anticipation on the fan's face as well as the fan's smiles and hearing them say, "Thank you!" afterward. Those memories will last a lifetime.

THE INVITATION

After winning the 1967 championship, the entire Ely Fagan team was invited by Bill Cox, Chairman of the Rochester-area American Legion Baseball, to a special victory celebration and dinner at the Mapledale Party House along with the Rochester Red Wings baseball team. What an experience it was being there among Red Wings players, having a chance to meet them, talk to them, and "break bread" together. Future Major League players were there, as was the Red Wings manager.

The city of Rochester and Rochester-area baseball fans were proud of its state champion, the Ely Fagan baseball team, and rolled out the red carpet to show appreciation for all that the team accomplished.

The invitation was special, and the Ely Fagan baseball team gladly accepted!

Richard Goodwin Sr.

APRIL 16th of the

43rd CONSECUTIVE YEAR OF

AMERICAN LEGION BASEBALL

1968

Congratulations! You are a member of the first team ever to win the Department of New York American Legion Baseball Championship. Every Legionnaire in Monroe County is proud of the Ely-Fagan team of 1967. The manner in which they conducted themselves in the Championship Game at Cooperstown and in the Regional play-offs for the National Championship.

You and the members of your team are to be honored at the Annual Dinner for the Rochester Red Wings sponsored by The Monroe County American Legion on Friday, April 26th at the Mapledale Party House, 1020 Maple Street, Rochester, New York.

We would like you to report at 6:00 P. M. to a room assigned for American Legion Baseball and Red Wing Players. You will be given instructions and your ticket at this time. Please complete the enclosed post card and mail promptly.

The dress for the occasion will be your "Sunday Best"

Most sincerely yours,

Bill

William J. Cox, Chairman
American Legion Baseball

The Ely Fagan Baseball Team Performance

Business performance, athletic performance, artistic performance . . . performance in general, is the result of many, various factors. One size doesn't fit all when it comes to performance because we, and the situations we find ourselves in, are all unique. The performance qualities we bring to the table, and what works for some may not work for others when it comes to performance outcomes and identifying performance cause and effect. But I think some generalizations can be made; I think there are some ingredients, factors, and qualities high-performing individuals have in common.

Certainly some, but not all characteristics and qualities that readily come to mind are: 1) "raw" or natural talent and ability, 2) overall health and well-being, 3) mental, physical, and emotional preparedness, 4) age and experience, 5) motivation, 6) determination, 7) attitude, 8) knowledge, and 9) environment—whether or not it's positive, supportive, neutral, or negative.

The Rush-Henrietta, New York, Ely Fagan American Legion State Championship team, coach, and players presented a special mix of talents and abilities, and those unique talents and abilities came together in the record-setting 1967 season. For sure, the game of baseball, by its very nature, combines both individual and team effort, and performance. When both individual and team effort, and performance are at their best, chances for success are at their highest. That's what happened in 1967, for the New

York State Ely Fagan Championship team and players. The individual and team efforts were extraordinary and at their best, victory in Cooperstown was the result and shared accomplishment.

SPRING TRAINING
WITH THE CARDINALS

For 25 years or so, Grandma and Grandpa traveled by car from Rochester, NY, to Florida for a winter vacation. Yes, winters were and still are cold in Rochester, and Gram and Grampa, along with many other northerners, valued several weeks in Florida's sunnier and warmer winter weather away from freezing temperatures and the accompanying ice and snow.

Grandma and Grandpa were baseball fans, and liked the New York Yankees and the St. Louis Cardinals Major League Baseball teams. When they traveled down to Florida, they made a point of visiting the Cardinals during their preseason spring training, and in 1964, they saw the Cardinals work out in St. Petersburg.

Not only did they watch the Cardinals players play, they also got to meet several of the players because way back then, the players made time to come over to some of the luckier fans to greet them, and even provide an autograph or 2—free of charge! This was a very special treat for any Cardinals fan, and Grandma and Grandpa relished the special opportunity to meet players, even if it was only for a minute or 2.

So, standing just outside the playing field next to the chain link fence, Grandma and Grandpa waited patiently to get an up-close glimpse of a player or 2, and their patience was promptly rewarded. They saw and met Red Schoendienst, then "Doc" Eberhardt stopped by to say, "Hello." They were thrilled to meet them. Both provided their autographs on the back of Grandma's beautiful picture-postcard of St. Petersburg beach. Then along came Branch Rickey and Stan "The Man" Musial. Both added their autographs to the back of Grandma's postcard, and Grandma snapped a camera-quick photo of the great Mr. Musial. What a special spring training day it was for both Grandma and Grandpa.

When Grandma and Grandpa arrived back home to Rochester, they showed me the postcard, the autographs, and picture of Stan Musial, and they decided to give me the postcard and picture! I have them to this day, and they have become a valued part of my baseball memorabilia collection.

As valuable as these items are now, it's the memory of it all that's most important to me. It's the memory of my beloved grandparents, their generosity and their love of family and the game of baseball, and it's the appreciation and gratitude I still hold for all those who were part of the Golden Age of Baseball back in the 1950s, and 1960s.

Stan Musial

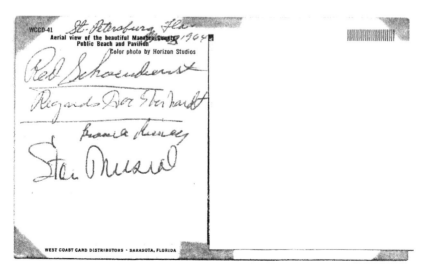

The Satchel
Paige Connection

The great baseball pitcher Satchel Paige was inducted into the National Baseball Hall of Fame in Cooperstown, New York, in August 1971. Anyone who ever had the privilege of seeing Satchel Paige pitch knew they were witnessing something very special. Satchel Paige was a phenomenon, and various baseball experts agree that Satchel Paige was one of the greatest pitchers of all time. He threw one pitch, a fastball, and he won most of his games throwing just that one pitch to hitters. Some have said Satchel's fastball was the fastest fastball of all-time. Simply put, his fastball was overpowering.

My grandfather, Carl, knew about Satchel Paige and his pitching accomplishments. And later in his baseball career, during the 1950s, Satchel pitched for several years with the AAA International League baseball team the Miami Marlins. The Miami Marlins played the Rochester Red Wings, and Grandpa Carl knew Satchel Paige would be coming to town, and that Satchel was scheduled to pitch. Grandpa Carl wanted me to see Satchel Paige pitch, so the day Satchel took the mound, Grandpa Carl and I were in our seats and eager to watch.

There was a close to capacity crowd that day, and Satchel was greeted with a standing ovation as he walked out to the mound. The first thing I noticed was Satchel's long, thin, lanky body. It seemed everything about him was long and lanky, including his feet and the spikes he wore. I was especially amazed by his arm length. When he stood tall, holding the ball between pitches, with his arms, hands, and fingers just hanging straight down from his shoulders, it appeared his hands hung all the way down to just below his knees!

Then, he wound up, lifted his left leg, and sprung forward toward home plate, and released the baseball toward the hitter. His windup seemed slow and easy, but his release was forceful, and the baseball rocketed past the batter, and into the catcher's mitt. Strike one! And so it went. Satchel struck out most of the hitters he faced, and as I recall, there were a number of foul balls hit one direction or the other. No hitter made solid contact with any of the pitches he threw. He was truly spectacular!

Some years later, my father met Satchel Paige just before Satchel was inducted into the National Baseball Hall of Fame. Dad was a multi-year, dedicated Little League Baseball District Administrator, and frequently needed to visit Williamsport, Pennsylvania—the Little League Baseball headquarters—for official meetings. Dad not only met Satchel Paige, but Satchel autographed one of dad's blank, Little League Baseball stationery letters. "Best Wishes from Satchel Paige."

Dad gave me Satchel's autograph, and I cherish it along with my vivid, lasting memory of watching Satchel Paige pitch in the 1950s, at Rochester's Norton Street location of Red Wing Stadium.

Little League Baseball

Williamsport   Pennsylvania

Baseball for Boys

June 5, 1971

District Administrator

Best wishes
from,
Satchel Paige

DAD

My father, Al Goodwin, grew up in Penfield, New York, in the 1920s–early 1940s. His father emigrated from Leeds, Great Britain to America, and he chose the Rochester, New York, area to be his new home. Grandfather Goodwin was a master cabinet maker and wood finisher, and he found work to utilize his expertise and skills at a piano manufacturer called The Aeolian-American Piano Corporation/the Piano Works factory, which was located in the small village of East Rochester where he worked for many years.

Dad excelled in soccer and played some baseball at Penfield High School. Shortly after graduating from high school, he enlisted in the US Army where he served during WWII. After the war, Dad and Mom decided to settle in East Rochester where they raised their 3 children, and where they ultimately resided their entire adult lives.

Dad worked hard. He always did. He worked as a metallurgist for a division of General Motors in Rochester, and after spending 30 years there, he retired at age 62. Unfortunately, Dad didn't enjoy much retirement time because he died from cancer merely 4 years later.

Dad was a good and generous man who put others first. He always helped around the house and did his best to provide for his family. He was caring, sharing, and genuinely loved others, and he did whatever he could to help others out. He also loved Rochester, and his home community of East Rochester. After arriving home from work, he'd help make dinners, help clean up, and then we'd hop in the car and off we'd go to baseball practices or games. (Having grown up during the Great Depression and living with very little, Dad told Mom he wanted to provide his children with good, daily, nutritious meals, and good clothes and shoes) We drove to so many baseball practices and games over the years, it was as though the car eventually knew where to go and when! He always tried to put Mom, my brother, sister, and me before himself, day in and day out, as long as he lived. As my lifelong friend, and former Ely Fagan teammate, Don Leege recently told me, "Your father was a good man who didn't have a bad bone in his body." Yes, that was my father.

Dad, along with many, many other fathers, mothers, and volunteers, plugged into the Little League program and devoted countless hours helping to make the program the best it could be. His passion to give and be involved, inspired and propelled him to become a leader of East Rochester's program, and then to become an area District Administrator of Rochester's overall Little League/Senior League program. He served Rochester as District Administrator for 11 years. Over those 11 years, he drove to, and attended, numerous Little League Administrative meetings in Williamsport, Pennsylvania, as Rochester's representative. And he was elected Deputy Mayor of East Rochester. While Deputy Mayor, East Rochester's 1965 Senior League team won the New York State Championship, and next year's 1966 team went all the way to become Senior League World Champions!

Dad's many contributions and volunteer efforts, to both the East Rochester and greater Rochester Little League programs are his lasting baseball legacy. While he was involved, all he ever did and tried to do was to help players, coaches, parents, and their representative communities have the best Little League programs and experiences possible. He worked hard to get along with people, and he expected people around him to get along with each other for the benefit of the Little Leaguers. Great Rochester and Ely Fagan pitcher Gary Junge referred to my father as Rochester's "Mr. Little League." I cannot disagree.

Ithaca College legendary Hall of Fame baseball Coach Carlton "Carp" Wood with my father, Al Goodwin, enjoying a pregame get-together on Ithaca's Freeman Field, circa May 1970.

The Rochester Red Wings and Red Wing Stadium

Growing up in the Rochester, New York, area, and playing baseball there in the 1950s and 1960s, was truly amazing. Baseball was a big deal. Little League, Babe Ruth League, Senior League, American Legion Baseball, and Muni baseball were in full swing, and an important part of family and community sports life come spring and summertime in Rochester. As I've mentioned, it was without question a "Golden Age" for amateur and youth baseball.

Surrounding all of this was the important influence of the Rochester Red Wings baseball team. The Red Wings were (and still are) Rochester's professional baseball presence. The Red Wings played (and still play) in the International League—at the Triple-A (1899 to present) level. Baseball history shows the Red Wings are 1 of 6 North American professional sport teams playing in the same city and league since the 1800s; the team is the oldest, continuously-operating sports franchise below the Major League level, and during the 1950s and 1960s, the Red Wings were the Triple-A affiliate and farm team for the St. Louis Cardinals, and subsequently, the Baltimore Orioles Major League teams. The Red Wings played in Red Wing Stadium, later to be renamed Silver Stadium, after Morrie Silver—a Rochester-area businessman who was instrumental in saving the Rochester Red Wings baseball franchise. In more recent times, the team moved from the Norton Street location to its current field, "Frontier Field" in the downtown Rochester area. Most recently, the team has become the Triple-A affiliate of the Washington Nationals Major League team.

It was especially thrilling as a 5-, 6-, 7-, and 8-year-old during the mid-1950s to go to Red Wings games, and especially to Sunday doubleheaders! Two games, not one! Double the fun. It was amazing and exciting just to walk the sidewalk up to the ticket booth, look up at the ticket booth person, buy the ticket, and hold the game ticket in my hand! Showing the ticket and walking through the turnstile came next. Then walking into the complex, finding the seat section and seat itself was the next step, and at that point, I could look out onto the beautiful, grassy field, the fences, and the huge, black center field scoreboard with the large clock perched on top. That huge, scoreboard clock made it easy to read the time. Flags waved in the breeze, and the upbeat, happy sound of organ music added to the pregame spirit and atmosphere. The grounds crew scurried about meticulously raking the infield dirt and lining the infield, outfield foul lines, and home plate areas. It was all glorious, and I never tired of watching pregame activities unfold in front of me. Watching batting practice and infield practice was the cherry on top! I loved to zero in on the players and coaches in their pregame activities. I watched them stretch, throw, catch, field ground balls and fly balls, and hit from the practice batting cage. Best I could, I observed their movements, activities, techniques, and skills, and learned plenty watching them. It was both inspirational and an invaluable baseball learning experience.

The food and drink concessions could be found down below. My grandmother, who loved the Red Wings, and who took me by bus transportation to those games, was comfortable letting me go down on my own to buy a slice of pizza, some peanuts or popcorn, or a hot dog, and some cotton candy! It was a different time back then; less risky, more people-friendly, and the only concern she or I had was whether or not I would remember how to get back to her and my seat! I was careful to note my comings and goings, landmarks, and my seating section and aisle number. I always got back without a hitch. And the more I did it, the more familiar I became with my comings and goings to the concession stands, no matter where we sat during games. It was a real confidence and independence builder. For me, a young baseball player and spectator, it was truly a growing experience, and veritable feast of Red Wings baseball, food and drink concessions, and game-related activities.

Each year during the mid-1950s, the big-league team . . . the St. Louis Cardinals . . . came to Rochester and Red Wing Stadium for an exhibition game. The stadium filled with fans, young and old, and all hoped for a glimpse of the Cardinals players. I can still see Stan "The Man" Musial standing near and leaning on the roof of the third base dugout, smiling, and looking up at the fans. The Rochester sports press was there, and flashbulbs popped everywhere near Stan "The Man," and the other Cardinals players! Young and old fans alike were thrilled the Cardinals came to town to grace the grounds of Red Wing Stadium, and to spend time with them!

There were many, many future Cardinals and Orioles big-league players, and big-league coaches, and managers who came through Rochester, and who first played or coached at Red Wing Stadium. I saw some of them, met some of them, and will always remember watching their amazing talents and memorable performances. The great Hall of Fame pitcher Bob Gibson first comes to mind. I remember seeing him seeking shelter and warmth in the cold, open air—in the bullpen area—out beyond the left field fence, where he and other pitchers, tried to get warm near a large, flame-spewing barrel. His baseball talents weren't confined to pitching, and it wasn't unusual for the Red Wings to call him in from the bullpen to pinch hit or pinch run. Then there was the great slugger Boog Powell. I remember witnessing Boog launch home run after home run. His homers were towering, rocket shots which went high over, and well beyond the right field fence, with some even clearing the right field light towers! He was big and powerful. I saw and heard his home run shots soar over the right field fence, eventually landing on some unsuspecting automobile, shattering the windshield, or denting the roof or hood! From my general admission seat, I could hear the impact of the ball as it hit the car or shattered the windshield glass! Hall of Famer Stan Musial passed through Rochester and the Red Wings too. And there was the great Hall of Fame player, coach, and manager Red Schoendienst. "Mr. Rochester Baseball" Joe Altobelli, smooth fielding first baseman, solid hitter, and super successful coach and manager played for the Red Wings and left a "forever" impact and influence on Rochester, and Rochester Red Wings baseball. I loved watching Joe Altobelli play first base. I was astounded by how he played the first base position with such precision and grace. He rarely, if ever, made an error, and he made the double play from his first base position to second base and back to first, look easy. What a talent! The Ripken family, Billy, Cal, Sr., and Cal, Jr., also passed through Rochester. Some others I saw play or manage in Rochester were Don Baylor, Mark Belanger, Paul Blair, Al Bumbry, Mike Epstein, Bobby Grich, Davey Johnson, and Earl Weaver. And I will never forget the wonderful memories the great former Red Wings player Luke Easter provided.

Big, Luscious "Luke" Easter was a legendary Rochester Red Wings player. Big Luke played Major League Baseball and, years prior to that, he played in the Negro leagues. He played at 6 feet 4 and around 240 pounds, he hit left-handed, and he provided some of the most memorable Red Wings players moments in Red Wings history! Luke is in the International Baseball League Hall of Fame. He hit line drive shots long and far, many sailing over the center field and right field fences. I rarely ever saw Luke hit a ball to left field. Opposing team outfielders played him deep . . . usually out by the warning track near the fence.

Luke was in his 40s to early 50s when he played in Rochester, and he started some games at his first base position. And if he wasn't in the starting lineup, he was in the dugout waiting to be called upon to come out to pinch hit. And pinch hit he did! Usually, he would get the nod to pinch hit late in the game. He frequently pinch hit in the bottom of the 9th inning, with runners on base, and 2 men out. He would emerge from the dugout, and then stride to the batters' warm up circle with several bats in hand, and he would swing them back and forth to warm up. The fans would chant "Luke," "Luke," "LUUUUKE!" Then, he'd enter the batter's box and settle in. What happened next was electric! The pitch would come in, and then Luke would swing. The sound of Luke's bat hitting the ball would be heard both inside and outside the ballpark! Then, the ball would leave his bat as though shot from a cannon and soar out of the ballpark. He would then, slowly and deliberately, round the bases with fans cheering wildly. Luke would come through for his team and all his fans. His hits were enormous game winners. Luke was the consummate, power hitting, clutch performer!

The Red Wings would hold youth baseball clinics at Red Wing Stadium from time to time, and on one occasion, our Senior League Baseball team was invited to Red Wing Stadium to work out with some of the Red Wings players. I ended up working with Luke Easter. Luke pitched to me, and I hit the ball hard, and he remarked something like, "Hey, kid, you can really hit." "Keep it up." Well, his words of encouragement meant a lot to me, and Luke's words inspired me to keep going in baseball! Yes, I guess Luke Easter, big number 36, was and still is one of my favorite Red Wings players (along with Joe Altobelli and Don Fazio), and for good reason!

I, and my fellow legion championship team teammates, had, on several occasions, played in baseball games at Red Wing Stadium. What a thrill it was to play on that big, historic, professional baseball field. We played all-star and championship games there, and the experiences were so special.

Yes, the Rochester Red Wings organization has been, and continues to be a positive sports presence and influence in the greater Rochester community. Red Wings baseball isn't just a spectator sport for young and old alike to enjoy, it is woven into the Rochester, New York, community and culture, and Red Wings baseball remains a lasting, vital part of the Rochester way of life. Under the continued leadership and dedication of Red Wings president, CEO, and COO Naomi Silver, General Manager Dan Mason, and because of the ongoing contributions of so many others, the rich tradition and legacy of Red Wings Triple-A baseball lives on.

THE ROCHESTER RED WINGS' BROADCASTERS

When the Ely Fagan American Legion Baseball players were in Little League, Babe Ruth League, and Senior League during the 1950s and early 1960s, we attended as many Rochester Red Wings games as we could. The Red Wings were Rochester's professional baseball team and the Triple-A affiliate of the St. Louis Cardinals Major League team. Naturally, many Rochester, New York, baseball fans, of all ages, were also fans of the Cardinals. The Red Wings showcased some amazing baseball talent and many, many exciting baseball games at the old Red Wing Stadium, which was located on Rochester's Norton Street. But when kids couldn't get to games, the next best thing was to listen to the play-by-play broadcasts by 2 former Rochester broadcasting legends, the great Tom Decker and Joe Cullinane.

Tom Decker broadcasted the Red Wings games from the mid-1950s into the 1960s, when Joe Cullinane took the helm and continued delivering radio broadcasts into the 1970s. Tom Decker followed Hall of Fame broadcaster Jack Buck. Jack Buck moved on to broadcast for the St. Louis Cardinals. When the Wings were playing out of town, the game action was transmitted to the broadcast team and then they relayed what happened to the radio listening audience. When a player hit a home run, we would hear a loud, crisp sound of "wood hitting wood" and then the announcers would say something like this: "There's a long fly ball hit deep to left field, it's hit high and deep, the left fielder is moving back near the warning track, near the fence, he's looking up, it's going, going, it's gone! It's a home run!" And then Joe Cullinane would add, "It's a White Owl Wallop!" That's what Joe Cullinane would say after each home run. "It's a White Owl Wallop!" And that's because one of the sponsors was White Owl Cigars!

We eagerly and intently listened to hear what Tom Decker and Joe Cullinane would say and how they would say it. Somehow, they found ways to make the broadcasts and game play-by-play action exciting and entertaining. There was never a dull moment, even when the games turned into pitchers' duels.

Yes, Rochester-area baseball players and fans were fortunate to have grown up around the Red Wings. We were also fortunate to have experienced baseball game broadcasts by the 2 Hall of Fame Rochester Red Wings announcers—Tom Decker and Joe Cullinane!

TIME WITH THE RED WINGS

In the early 1990s, I lived and worked near Rochester, New York, and could drive to Red Wing Stadium/Silver Stadium from my home in around 30 minutes. It was at that time I connected with the Rochester Red Wings. A handful of the Red Wings players frequented my business and over time, I enjoyed getting to know them, and really enjoyed talking baseball with them. I especially enjoyed talking to former Red Wing Bobby Dickerson. Bobby had experienced a terrific, professional playing career. Other players I got to know were Eddie Yacopino, Anthony Telford, Jim Poole, and Doug Jennings.

I told Bobby Dickerson I had played some baseball in high school and college, and he surprised me by inviting me to come out to Red Wing Stadium/Silver Stadium to join in with practice, throw the ball around with players, and just have a good time. I was in my 40s and hadn't touched a baseball in years, but it sounded like fun, so I took him up on the offer! When I arrived the first day, I parked in a VIP space near the field, gave security my name, walked into the ballpark and then down onto the field, and joined the players. I had played on the Red Wings' field several times in high school, baseball tournament play, Ely Fagan American Legion Baseball competition, and Municipal Baseball competition, but not with the Red Wings. The manager of the Red Wings then was former big-league player, and current roving instructor for the Chicago White Sox, Jerry Narron, and the pitching coach was Steve Luebber. They were okay with me being there with them on the field, among the players, and I settled in with the team in its practices. Legendary Red Wings player Joe Altobelli, Rochester's "Mr. Baseball," who was the former Orioles manager of the World Champion 1983 Baltimore Orioles baseball team, would occasionally visit practices and come onto the field and into the dugout. "Alto" was the smoothest-fielding first baseman I ever saw. During one of the practices, he came onto the field, and into the dugout, to share a hitting story with Manager Narron, Rich Dauer (visiting Orioles coach), Red Wings player Doug Jennings, and I happened to be there too. Joe recalled a batting slump he'd been in early in his professional baseball career, and he explained how he worked his way out of it. He was hitting around .235 and didn't know what to do. One day, he accidentally hit a pitch down, onto the top inside area of his right foot resulting in some serious pain and discomfort. As he explained, he couldn't put any weight onto his right foot (he was a left-handed hitter) because of the injury, and his coach asked Joe if he'd like to take himself out of the lineup to rest his injury. Joe said he wanted to keep playing and play he did! Because of the injury, he couldn't place much weight forward in his batting stance onto his right foot, thus forcing him to keep his weight back in his stance on his left foot. The result of the weight shift, according to him, was a career saver! He said it was the best injury he ever had because he learned how to keep his weight back in his stance, he began hitting again, and he raised his batting average from .235 to .325! We all enjoyed his story; we knew the point he was making, and we thoroughly enjoyed the interesting and entertaining way he made it! Joe had a fine professional playing career, he was a super-smooth fielding, nimble first baseman with a strong and accurate throwing arm, and he was a dependable, powerful, consistent, and "clutch" pinch hitter.

That summer, I threw batting practice to many of the Red Wings players during their regular practices, and I really enjoyed it. I spent extra, individual time throwing BP to Red Wings player Doug Jennings. He wanted me to throw to him, so he and I arranged our schedules so I could come out to the stadium to throw batting practice just to him. Doug was a powerful left-handed hitter, and since I threw left-handed, he saw it as an important opportunity to see more left-handed pitching. He'd call me at home, I'd hop in the car, and in 45 minutes, I'd be on the field throwing BP to him. Then after he hit, and we recovered all his batted balls, he'd throw to me and I'd hit! It was great fun hitting baseballs again, hitting with his bat (which was really a bit too long and heavy for me!), hearing the sound and echo of the bat contacting the baseball, and then watching the ball travel in the air to the outfield with some batted balls rolling to the warning track and against the right field fence. Doug hit some balls out over the fence in right field, and I was amazed by his bat speed, strength, and power!

When I was at the Red Wings practices, I was also invited to put on my old, first baseman's mitt, and participate in infield and outfield drills! It was like old times, catching ground balls and fly balls, taking throws from the infielders, and making outfield throws to second base, third base, and to the catcher at home plate.

I became known by players, security, and attendants around the stadium and parking lots, and I could park next to the stadium, walk right in, and watch Red Wings games free of charge, and I was able to sit wherever I wanted to! Typically, I'd sit directly behind home plate in the lower level—very good seats—near the players' families, scouts, and Baltimore personnel. A couple of times, I sat near Hall of Famer and Major League Baseball executive Frank Robinson, and on several occasions, I sat near former big leaguer Wally Moon. Mr. Moon charted information about the Red Wings and opposing players. And one game component he was especially interested in was assisting and coaching right-handed hitters to teach them how to hit the ball to right field, behind the runner who was advancing from first base, to second base in order to advance the runner further to third base. During the games, he'd ask me what I thought about certain players and game situations. He would involve me in the game we were watching, and he seemed interested in what I had to say. One night, during one of the Red Wings games, he held up his hands to me and said, "Look at these fingers!" I looked and saw swollen knuckles and bent fingers. He then went on to say, "I've broken these fingers playing baseball, I played with broken fingers, and I never missed a game because of my broken fingers!" He then made a comment about the difference between older baseball players and modern players. He pointed out a few of the players and said, "Those players missed games and went on the DL (Disabled List) because of simple hangnails!" All in all though, when I was at Red Wings practices and games, I was amazed by the speed, size, and strength of the players. I truly enjoyed the time I spent with the players, and I was fortunate to have had those experiences. Thanks, Bobby Dickerson!

As mentioned before, growing up in the Rochester, New York, area and going to the Red Wings games over the years was a terrific experience. As a kid, I got to see some amazing baseball players come through Rochester. One was the great Bob Gibson. I saw Bob Gibson pitch, and he was such a fine hitter and runner, he'd usually also help his cause when he came to the plate, and when he was running the bases. It wasn't unusual to see him come in from the bullpen to pinch hit, and he'd often come through by getting a base hit. Some other Red Wings I saw play that come to mind are: big Boog Powell, big Luke Easter, Ozzie Virgil, brothers Dick and Dave Ricketts, Bob Keegan, Del Rice, Ray Sadecki, Pete Ward, Ruben Amaro, Tim McCarver, Tommy Burgess, Cal Browning, Gene Green, Cot Deal, Wally Shannon, Jim Frey, Ray Washburn, Cal Ripken, Fred Valentine, Herm Starrette, Jim Palmer, Gary Geiger, Roy Smalley, Paul Blair, Don Baylor, Mark Belanger, Steve Bilko, Steve Demeter (who hit the longest home run I ever saw—it traveled over the huge clock which was mounted way up at the very top of the distant centerfield scoreboard), Eddie Stevens, Davey Johnson, Bobby Grich, and Ithaca College Athletics Hall of Famer Don Fazio. For many years, and throughout the 1950s, the Red Wings were the Triple-A

Minor League club for the St. Louis Cardinals. Then the Wings became the Triple-A Minor League team of the Baltimore Orioles, followed by the Minnesota Twins, and nowadays, as mentioned before, they are the Triple-A International League affiliate for the Washington Nationals. Usually, once during the season, the Major League teams would visit Rochester to play the Wings in an exhibition game. It was a very exciting event and fans loved it! The stands were usually packed to capacity when the big-league clubs came to town. The press was there with their old-fashioned flashbulb cameras. Again, on one occasion, I remember seeing a multitude of light bulbs flash and pop in staccato-like rhythm when sports reporters and cameramen took pictures of a smiling Stan "The Man" Musial, who graciously stood for them just outside the visitor's dugout while holding and resting several of his bats on his left shoulder. All eyes were on Stan Musial as he stepped up and out of the dugout!

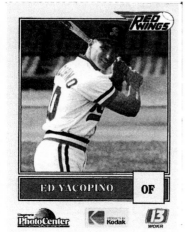

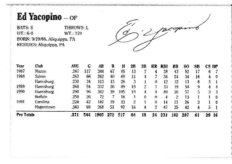

Ed Yacopino — OF

BATS: S THROWS: L
HT.: 6-0 WT.: 170
BORN: 9/19/66, Aliquippa, PA
RESIDES: Aliquippa, PA

Year	Club	AVG	G	AB	R	H	2B	3B	HR	RBI	BB	SO	SB	CS	HP
1987	Macon	.247	117	344	67	85	13	2	4	38	43	52	17	6	7
1988	Salem	.263	66	262	40	69	11	4	7	34	24	34	16	4	0
	Harrisburg	.230	34	113	13	26	3	1	0	12	12	13	6	5	1
1989	Harrisburg	.264	94	337	36	89	19	2	7	33	19	50	9	4	1
1990	Harrisburg	.290	96	362	39	105	19	4	4	89	26	57	5	3	3
	Buffalo	.250	26	72	7	18	1	0	0	4	2	13	1	1	0
1991	Carolina	.224	42	187	19	33	2	1	0	14	21	26	3	1	0
	Hagerstown	.343	69	268	51	92	16	4	2	47	35	42	4	5	1
Pro Totals		**.271**	**544**	**1905**	**272**	**517**	**84**	**18**	**24**	**231**	**182**	**287**	**61**	**29**	**16**

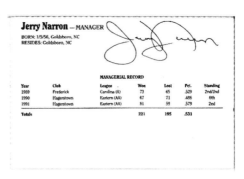

Jerry Narron — MANAGER

BORN: 1/5/56, Goldsboro, NC
RESIDES: Goldsboro, NC

		MANAGERIAL RECORD				
Year	Club	League	Won	Lost	Pct.	Standing
1989	Frederick	Carolina (A)	73	65	.529	2nd/2nd
1990	Hagerstown	Eastern (AA)	67	71	.486	6th
1991	Hagerstown	Eastern (AA)	81	59	.579	2nd
Totals			**221**	**195**	**.531**	

Paying the Price

*"You can't sit on a lead and run a few plays into the
line and just kill the clock. You've got to throw the ball
over the darn plate and give the other man his chance.
That's why baseball is the greatest game of them all."*
—Earl Weaver

My high school football coach and gym teacher used to preach,
"If you want to win, you have to pay the price!" He'd also tell
players, "Winners never quit, and quitters never win!" Well, I am
guessing he heard those expressions before, somewhere else, and
decided he'd use them as motivational tools. He was the ultimate
decider about what the "price" was we needed to pay and what
constituted "quitting." He was demanding, uncompromising,
and unforgiving in his roles of coach and gym teacher. He ended
up coaching high school football for many years, he amassed
many wins and relatively few losses, and he and his record
became legendary. He accomplished what most coaches didn't, or
couldn't, because he figured out how to get the most from his
players, by coaching players to get the most out of themselves.

The Ely Fagan players paid a price to achieve excellence in
baseball. They spent years and years learning the game of baseball
and honing their skills. They practiced consistently, and gave 100
percent effort each and every time they took the field. At times
they played hurt because they cared about contributing to the
team and the coach who believed in them. Their Ely Fagan coach,
Mr. Petersen, cared about each player, and expected his players to
give it their all. He was enthusiastic, upbeat, encouraging, sup-

portive, and he knew his players so well, he knew what to say and do no matter the situation. He respected his players, and his players respected him in return. He wasn't intimidating. He was inspiring. He didn't need to push his players around. He was accepting of his players and others around him. He was the consummate coach. Together, the players and Coach Petersen made magic on the baseball field. The magic they made resulted in winning the 1967 New York State American Legion Baseball championship. No Rochester, New York, team before or after—spanning close to 100 years—has done that, and now it remains a record and accomplishment that may never again be matched.

THERE'S NO JOB TOO TOUGH!

Most of us have been in challenging situations at work or at home that required everything we could possibly muster to seek and identify solutions, and then move on from there. When I was in the US Army many years ago, the motto of our unit was, "There's no job too tough!" Believe me, there were times when the jobs were tough, but being Army trained helped provide the resolve to see things through.

Playing sports for many years, particularly the game of baseball, also equipped me with a certain "resolve" to see things through; to have that never quit attitude. Lots happened over a 9-inning game, and there were usually abundant opportunities to get a big hit, score a go-ahead or game-winning run, or make a good play in the field. The question became, "Could I come through and get the job done?" and "Will I come through for the team and help the team win?" Most often, the answer was, "Yes I can," and "Yes I will!" Coming through in an assortment of situations, and in a clutch, taught me and others, "There's no job too tough!"

THE TALK AT THE
WORLD TRADE CENTER

In the mid-1980s, I was invited by the American Management Association to give a talk at the World Trade Center. The topic for my address was, "How to effectively market insurance and annuity products in banks." At that time, banks were becoming more marketing and sales oriented, and they were interested in knowing more about how to do it. The bank I worked for in New York was a leader in annuity and insurance sales at that time, and I was happy to share what I knew, what we did, and how we did it. My audience was comprised of bank and insurance executives from around the United States.

The talk was scheduled to begin at 8 a.m., and I got up early so I could travel into the city, get to the World Trade Center, find the auditorium location, and settle in. I took an early train into New York, and then a cab from Grand Central Station to the World Trade Center, and arrived just as the sun was rising. I stepped out of the cab and viewed the size and scope of the buildings facing me. It was an awesome sight. I entered my building and was astounded by the size of space, and the marble that adorned the columns and walls around me. I found the elevator bank and up I went, got off at my floor, and walked to and entered the auditorium to arrange my papers at the podium, check the microphone, and ready myself.

The talk went well, but I could have done better. As a banker and college teacher, I had given talks to staff and students many times before and was comfortable doing it, however this was different. I found it a bit daunting to face a room filled with unfamiliar faces. But I grew from the experience, learned from it, and looking back, I am glad I did it. Afterward, I was treated to a tour of the tower, and I was escorted onto the top outside deck, and from there I could look out in every direction and see for many miles into the distance. It was an amazing sight and experience I will always remember.

In baseball, when a hitter steps into the batter's box, he faces a pitcher and a thrown ball, and much of what happens is unknown. Where will the pitched ball be thrown? Will the pitch be a fastball, a curve, an off-speed pitch, or something else? The challenge for hitters is to do what it takes to hit the ball hard, hit the ball long, or walk, but not to strike out. Hitters need to focus, be confident and skilled, know how to adjust, and swing at the right time, and make solid contact with the baseball.

Looking back, I am convinced playing baseball—being successful at playing baseball—helped prepare me for that World Trade Center talk. Sure, I was nervous, but that practice and preparation helped me conquer the uncertainty, and get the job done. As a hitter and infielder, I was similarly prepared to do my job on the baseball field, and that preparation helped me come through and meet the uncertainty and challenges presented in game situations when I played. Yes, I believe playing the game of baseball successfully helped me in all my life endeavors, including the challenges presented during my years of US Army military service.

It's an Honest Game

Maybe above all, the game of baseball is intended to be an honest game, to be played honestly by players. That's the way it was way back in 1967, when the Ely Fagan team played. Some of the performance enhancing activities and concepts back then for that team and players were extra baseball practice, dedication, consistency, strength training and occasional weightlifting, eating nutritiously, getting adequate rest, striving for excellence, and wanting to win. No performance enhancing drugs (PEDs)! Let me repeat . . . NO performance enhancing drugs!

Now we know that since then, in the decades that followed, PEDs have been used by some players in professional baseball, even players in the Major Leagues. We now know and recognize that use of PEDs cheapened the game of baseball, and it further cheapened a drug-using player's baseball performance. Users of PEDs were, and will continue to be, known as cheaters. Because baseball is intended to be an honest game, there has never been a legitimate place for PED users and cheaters. Whether the game is played by professionals or amateurs, the game of baseball has no room for players' performance enhancement through the use of PEDs. Period!

It's been said big money contributed to the player dishonesty, cheating, and the artificial performance enhancement through the use of drugs. I've heard players justified their use of PEDs in order to gain a competitive advantage over other players and the competition by artificially increasing their own levels of performance. Better performance equaled better pay. Right? NO! That's just plain wrong.

The Ely Fagan baseball team played our best and never cheated. Never. The Ely Fagan team represented what was good in baseball, and what was honest in sports. Players were good citizens both on and off the field. We competed fairly and honestly. We were gentlemen, good sports, and we always followed the rules of the game. Our parents, friends, and the communities we represented were proud of us, and our conduct.

The Ely Fagan players, coach, and manager respected the game of baseball and recognized it needed to be played honestly and with integrity, and that's exactly what we did.

DESTINY

I've heard it said, "No one controls his or her own life destiny with total or absolute certainty."

I think one comes to realize the accuracy of that statement the longer one lives. What person can predict, with 100 percent certainty, his or her own life journey? Who knows for sure what life's ups and downs will be? I have seen people change their life's outcome in a matter of seconds by one good or poor decision they've made. I've seen people prosper through no effort of their own while I've also seen industrious people lose it all through events they had no control over. Yes, we can and do control the best we can to provide some sense of life order and certainty, but will we ever truly be able to fully eliminate the unexpected and unforeseen?

The Ely Fagan baseball team won the New York State Championship in 1967, but could you say this was their destiny?

The 1966 Ely Fagan baseball team was a very good team, and they won most of their league games with their superior pitching, hitting, and fielding. They were confident as they began their tournament play and won their games in the early tournament rounds. They believed they were capable of making it to the New York State championship. Everything looked positive for them until they played a team from the Buffalo, New York area. That Buffalo-area team ended up beating the Ely Fagan team, and so the Buffalo team moved on in tournament play. Ely Fagan was eliminated.

To this day, some 1966 Ely Fagan players scratch their heads and wonder what happened. Why didn't they beat the Buffalo team? Was the Buffalo team that much better?

A couple of the 1966 players remember the Buffalo players came to play dressed in different uniforms. The uniforms signified that each player played on a different team, so it appears they were an all-star team comprised of the best players from all the various Buffalo-area American Legion teams. So looking back, the 1966 Rush-Henrietta Ely Fagan team—not a Rochester-area, hand-picked, all-star team—ended up playing against, and then losing to, a Buffalo city-wide, all-star team! If so, if that was indeed the case, it wouldn't have been fair or right. And if so, the 1966 Ely Fagan team would have found themselves in an unfair, competitive game situation. Was that their "destiny?"

Who knows! But one thing that can be shown and not disputed . . . the 1967 Ely Fagan team won the New York State Championship fair and square. They were one team comprised of one terrific team manager, one great, inspiring, and motivational coach, 2 young, energetic and dependable batboys, an amazing, fair-minded, and judicious scorekeeper, numerous supportive and caring family and friends from the Rochester community, and 14 truly dedicated and talented baseball players who played their hearts out!

Was it "destiny" that propelled the 1967 team to Cooperstown and the New York State Championship? Who knows! But maybe, just maybe, "destiny" did play a role in the team's success after all.

IS THE GAME THE SAME?

We've already touched on what it was like to play baseball in upstate New York back in the 1950s. We could meet with our neighborhood friends, hop on our bikes with our bats and mitts resting on or over our handlebars, and peddle over to the baseball field for a fun day of baseball playing. We were young then, in the age range of 5 to 11, and our moms and dads encouraged us to get out of the house, get with our friends, and play ball! The sunshine and fresh air felt so good. The rules were clear, and we followed them every time we played. This was unstructured play, and we saved the structured team practices, play, and official, sanctioned Little League games for the early evenings. Each player had his unique style of play. Parents and coaches stood back, watched, encouraged, and supported, but they didn't interfere with the players' natural development as baseball players. There wasn't a one-size-fits-all approach back then, and we all were given the opportunity to play naturally in ways that felt and worked best for us.

I guess you could say the game of baseball was simple back then, and it was without much analysis and science behind it. We chewed the very sugary, sweet tasting, pink-colored, bubblegum that came inside the little baseball card packs we bought. The gum tasted so good, although it wasn't the best thing for our teeth, and we could blow enormous bubbles when we chewed several pieces of gum at the same time. We never heard of steroids back then. We never heard the phrase, "Performance enhancing drugs" when we were kids. No, back then, competition was pure, and eye-hand coordination, size, and performance were God-given as well as the result of consistent practice.

Of course, things changed. When we were playing Little League Baseball in the 1950s, most professional baseball players didn't make a lot of money, and they needed to have jobs in the off-season to help make ends meet. Later on in the 1960s, professional baseball players began to make lots more money playing the game. In more recent times, some of the better players make many, many millions of dollars playing baseball. Getting and maintaining a competitive edge over other players became paramount, and some of the players resorted to taking or using performance enhancing drugs (PEDs) in order to do it. They cheated, and those who have been caught cheating have paid a high price for doing so. Science and analytics have now become mainstays in baseball. Radar guns are used to track pitch velocity. Pitches thrown to batters are counted, and when pitchers reach a certain pitch count number, they are taken out of games, and replaced by relief pitchers who come in from the bullpen. Strength training, stretching, and nutrition are closely monitored. Baseball gear has improved. Bats, balls, and gloves are much better now. The fields of play are in better shape. The infield dirt, grass, and the outfield area are manicured. There aren't many "bad" hops caused by stones and pebbles in the infield dirt areas because the stones and pebbles have been removed! When we played back in the 1950s, bad hops were part of the game. There's artificial turf now. There wasn't artificial turf on our baseball fields. Today's hitters wear all sorts of protective equipment including batting gloves, while our protective equipment consisted of helmets only, and we would reach down and rub dirt in our hands to improve our grip on the bat. Also, there's the various rule changes, like having designated hitters and automatic intentional walks.

Nowadays, batters seem to be coached differently and encouraged to hold their bats and hands certain ways to help improve their hitting efficiency and effectiveness. Players today are generally bigger, stronger, and faster. I could go on and on about the differences, but to sum it up, baseball playing today has become more sophisticated and analytical. Is it more fun? Maybe, and maybe not, but from where I'm sitting, I've got to believe that the game of baseball was generally more fun to play back in the 1950s and 1960s, and it was played honestly. We played because of the love of the game, and not for the love of the money.

2 MEMORABLE PLAYS

I worked for a bank in Mount Vernon, New York, for many years and one of my bank colleagues was a big New York Yankees fan. In addition to his bank job, he worked nights as a security supervisor for the Yankees at their home games. Every so often, he'd invite me to come out to see a game, and I'd drive down to the "old" Yankee Stadium and see the Yankees in action. It was a real treat, and I'll always remember those experiences and seeing 2 remarkable plays.

The first play involved Reggie Jackson, who was playing right field. We were sitting all the way down the right field line near the corner of the right field fence. The opposing team batter hit a line drive down the right field line that rolled into the right field corner just below where we were sitting. Reggie ran to the ball while the batter was running toward second base. Reggie picked up the ball at just about the time the runner reached second base and decided to try for a triple. The runner committed to try for third base, and Reggie committed to throwing him out. Reggie reared back, and with full force, launched his long throw to third. I couldn't believe what I then saw. Reggie's rifle throw—which traveled in a straight line—arrived precisely to third base before the runner got there, and the third baseman snagged Reggie's throw and then tagged the sliding runner out! It was unbelievable! We remember Reggie Jackson for his tape measure home runs, and for being "Mr. October," but I'll also remember him for having one of the strongest and most accurate outfielder throwing arms in baseball history.

The second play involved Bill Buckner. The Red Sox baseball team was in town to play the Yankees. I sat in the lower seating section at field level just behind and near the Red Sox third base dugout. As I looked out to the home plate area from where I sat, I noticed the field was actually above me! I was looking up at the hitter. Bill Buckner, a left-handed batter, stepped into the batter's box to face left-handed pitcher Dave Righetti. Righetti threw a sharp breaking ball, which came in low and outside. Buckner bent down and reached his bat out to meet the ball, he snapped and rolled his wrists and hands, and made solid contact with the ball. The next thing I saw — and I saw it clearly — was Buckner unbelievably hitting a low line drive that traveled like a rocket over the right field fence. From the time Buckner hit it, I estimate it took between 2 to 3 seconds for the ball to travel over the right field fence. He hit a shot, and how he was able to reach out, and just flick his bat onto the ball, and generate such power was truly amazing.

ARE YOU PHIL NIEKRO?

Just when I thought baseball was in my distant past, I found myself in a shopping center parking lot and being asked if I was a Hall of Fame pitcher!

Several years ago, my wife and I retired to a very nice community near the Georgia Mountains, and we discovered it's the same community where the late, Hall of Fame pitcher Phil Niekro called home. There's a street named after him and we'd driven on it many times, and my wife and I are pretty sure we once spotted him in a nearby coffee shop sitting and enjoying a fresh cup of coffee.

So one early morning, after we had just finished our grocery shopping, I was loading the groceries into the back of my car when I noticed another car slowly coming my way through the parking lot. As it approached, I wondered why it was approaching me, and what was the driver doing? The car stopped next to me, and the older driver rolled down his window, looked at me and asked, "Are you Phil Niekro?" His question caught me by surprise, so I thought a few seconds to try and remember who I was, and realized I wasn't Phil Niekro, and replied, "No, I'm not Phil Niekro." I then replied, "But if I was Phil Niekro, I'd give you my autograph!" Then he said, "I have Phil Niekro's autograph already . . . You look just like Phil Niekro. You're about his height, and your hair looks like the way he has his hair!" He finally realized and accepted I wasn't Phil Niekro so then he said, "Well, you seem like a very nice man. It was good talking to you." Then, he drove away, and my wife and I shared a smile and a chuckle! He made our day because for a few minutes, he thought I was a Hall of Famer! He actually believed I was the great knuckleball pitcher Philip Henry "Knucksie" Niekro!

WAS THE ELY FAGAN
TEAM THE BEST EVER?

It's now approaching 100 years of American Legion Baseball being played in the Rochester, New York, area. More than a thousand teams, and many thousands of players, have played Rochester-area American Legion Baseball over those many years. There have been many talented American Legion players, including the great Rochester-area pitcher and Major League star, the late Johnny Antonelli, yet other than the Ely Fagan 1967 team and players, no other American Legion player or team from the Rochester area can claim a New York State American Legion Baseball Championship. Was the 1967 Ely Fagan team Rochester's best Legion team ever? Maybe so. That team was, and still is, the most successful. Our 1967 winning percentage and record and our New York State Championship remain unmatched. And as has already been cited, most of the 1967 Ely Fagan players went on to become outstanding college and university baseball players, and Don Leege and Gary Junge went even further and played pro ball. That player record is truly outstanding and reflects the extensive and true talent of the team.

THE INDOOR TRACK

In my recent book, *Running Life Matters*, I write about my 45 years of running, and some of the life insights and inspiration running has provided. My book also includes some remarkable, motivational, and informational stories from friends and runners I have known over the years. Besides sharing a common bond, and a love for running, we also share the common characteristic of being strivers. We strive to overcome, to meet and exceed personal, and running goals and objectives, and we continue to keep going the best we can, even when faced with adversity.

Why did I become a runner? Well, several years after completing my military service and returning home to the USA, I found myself needing to find something sports related to do. I saw the sport of running had taken hold across America, so I thought I would give it a try. I was working in Mount Vernon, New York, and I joined the local Mount Vernon YMCA, which was conveniently located right around the corner from my workplace. It wasn't fancy, but it offered what I was looking for, including an indoor track. I bought an inexpensive pair of racing flats, and the rest is history. I began walking around the indoor track, then I mixed walking with jogging, and eventually I was able to jog or run my entire workout. I needed to run 22 laps around the track to complete one mile, and I was able to clock 4 to 5 miles on some training days. Yes, it was monotonous at times, and even boring, but that little indoor track helped me get the work in and the job done. After gaining some runner confidence, I decided to take my running outdoors, and from that point on, I became a dedicated and consistent outdoor runner. Little did I know at the time, I'd still be running 45 years later. That little indoor track helped me get started, and I remember those early days of running with great fondness and gratitude.

What does running have to do with baseball? Well, the game of baseball also provided many life lessons including that "never give in" and "try your best" attitude and work ethic. As baseball players, my teammates and I did the best we could, we tried to win, we challenged ourselves to improve at practices and in every game. In running, athletes drive to the finish line, and in baseball, players give it their all for the entire 9 innings. In both running and baseball, athletes don't give up but instead they persevere from start to finish. Yes, baseball is a team sport played by individuals, and the sport of running can become a great substitute sport for individual athletes like former baseball players when they can no longer field teams, hit, throw, or run the bases like they used to. Clearly, the sports of running and baseball are different, but I found playing baseball helped me understand the competitive aspects of running, and being a baseball player ultimately helped me become a successful, lifelong runner. Maybe there's an indoor or outdoor track somewhere just waiting for you.

THE GENESEE RIVER

The old and beautiful Genesee River flows from Pennsylvania through Rochester, New York, and into Lake Ontario. Over the course of history, it has carved its way down and through land areas, creating scenic settings and majestic views generations of people have enjoyed. The Rochester-area Genesee Valley Park is one such place. Thousands of picnickers, walkers, joggers, and others have recreated there over the years, and it has also provided places for baseball to be played. One such baseball field was nestled near the Genesee River and from home plate, a hitter could look out and beyond the right field area and see the flowing river far off in the distance. A left-handed hitter could only dream of hitting a ball far enough to reach the riverbank located far away and down the right field line.

Legend has it, one left-handed slugger amazingly did hit a ball that carried into the air, on the fly, the entire distance from home plate into the Genesee River. The distance of that Herculean poke was estimated to be well over 350 feet. That hitter was a former Rush-Henrietta pitching and hitting star, and former professional baseball player, the late Billy Rouse. Rouse was big, strong, and the home run he hit into the river—his Boog Powell-like blast—is still remembered and talked about by old-timers in the Rochester baseball community.

But there was another. Former 1967 Ely Fagan outfielder, and Auburn University star player and powerful hitter Joey Haefner also hit one into the river. His spectacular home run "bounced" in, but the ball came close to making it all the way on the fly.

Yours truly also hit one into the river in Rochester Muni baseball play, but my long home run merely bounced and rolled in.

Yes, the historic Genesee River is quite a site to see, as it passes to and through the Rochester area. It is also a site to watch a right fielder chase after a hit ball and come up empty handed because the ball has traveled far over his head and ended up in the water. Rouse, along with former 1967 Ely Fagan players Haefner and myself, are among a select group of left-handed hitters to have experienced it.

THE HITTER'S PLEDGE

As I take my place in the batter's box, no matter who the pitcher is, I will believe in my hitting ability, remain confident, and I will hit the ball hard, do my job, and I will never think I won't.

Thank You, Baseball

"Losers blame others, but winners don't blame.
Winners and leaders choose to live responsibly and
hold themselves accountable for their actions."
–Richard Goodwin, Sr.

The game of baseball is a wonderful game both because of its simplicity and its complexity. The rules are relatively simple, they are stable—9 players on each team, 9 innings in each game, 3 outs per inning, the team with the most runs scored, wins the game, etc.—but what happens after the ball is pitched is unknown, and the results are always unique and different. No 2 pitched balls are ever identical, no 2 hit balls are ever the same, and both batters and fielders alike do their best to prepare for whatever might happen and anticipate what they will do at any given time, and in any given situation before, during, or after the baseball has been pitched. Reaction times are split second. Batters have little time to decide what they will do when the pitched ball comes their way. Pitchers rear back and throw to the catcher's target, trying their best to overpower batters or surprise them with a variety of pitches to keep batters off balance. Fielders prepare mentally by visualizing and anticipating what they will do when the batted ball comes their way. Baseball games will always provide elements of unpredictability, moments of drama, suspense, and excitement. Maybe then, in some ways, understanding the game of baseball and playing the game of baseball helps us to better prepare for, understand, and effectively handle some of life's wins, losses, ups, and downs.

"Thank You, Baseball," and thanks to the National and New York State American Legion Baseball programs, from each of the 1967 New York State Champion Ely Fagan American Legion players. Because of the opportunities you gave us to play American Legion Baseball, we learned important life lessons. We learned about sportsmanship, responsibility, accountability, sacrifice, teamwork, and leadership, and that helped us to go on to become better citizens, husbands, fathers, and grandfathers.

Some Final Thoughts

The players on the Ely Fagan team grew up in simpler times. We didn't have computers, cell phones, video games, or social media, but we did have party-line phone connections, and face-to-face communication. We walked, ran, and rode our bikes all over town, and we raced outside to get as much fresh air, sunshine, and exercise as we could pack into each and every day, as our time and responsibilities allowed. We didn't have as many other activities to choose from, and we didn't have anywhere near the number of distractions there are today. Nowadays, of course, kids can pick and choose from an abundance of things to do. Times are different. We grew up in communities which were, for the most part, safe and supportive, and our parents didn't worry much about where we were, who we were with, or what we were doing. Our parents knew our friends, and our friends' parents, and together they all established a comfort level and mutual trust. Back then, we and our parents were interested in having good, clean fun. Times weren't perfect but they were really, really good. We learned early on that it wasn't mostly about money, material things, or having or getting more. The material things in life didn't seem to matter as much as relationships and friendships did. We learned how to be self-reliant, cooperative, and productive, young American citizens. We learned about rules and laws, and the difference between right and wrong. Although we developed a strong sense of liberty and independence, we also learned the meanings of fairness, honesty, duty, responsibility, and sacrifice. We learned how to be patient and respectful of the elderly. We learned to wait in line, knowing our turn would eventually come.

Most of the Ely Fagan players who decided to go to college after high school were "the first college generation" or the first in their families to ever do so. Our parents and grandparents were excited for us, and happy we would have educational opportunities they never had. They believed—and, for the most part, they were right about this—we would have better jobs and have better incomes than they did as a result of having a good college education. Our parents and grandparents sacrificed so we would have a chance to learn more and prosper. Bobby Porta became a very popular, and successful high school math teacher. Don Leege became a senior bank executive and enjoyed a long and successful career in commercial banking. Bill Kreger, Chuck Glaza, Joe and Andy Haefner, Gary Junge, Rene Piccarreto, and Rich Petersen all became managers, executives, business leaders, or business owners. Additionally, Rene has taught college business, marketing, and management courses for many years. Al Pannoni and Ralph Clapp devoted their adult lives to education, and both became successful teachers and high school Hall of Fame coaches. And similar results and successes hold true for my former Ithaca College baseball teammates.

Yes, the sacrifices and investments our parents, grandparents, coaches, teachers, and communities made for us have paid off because those important values and lessons have been passed forward. We've passed many of the things they taught and modeled for us along to our children and grandchildren, and they now live on through them. Again, we send our forever thanks to our moms, dads, grandmas, grandpas, former teachers, and coaches! You, and what you did, will always matter.

And yes, baseball life—our baseball lives—will always matter.

Epilogue

The Ely Fagan American Legion Post #1151 merged with the Stevens-Connor Post in 2020, so it is now known as the Ely Fagan-Stevens-Connor Post #1151. For many, many years, both Rochester-area legion posts—in conjunction with state and the national American Legion platforms and initiatives—have worked tirelessly and continuously to provide targeted support to the great Rochester-area veterans, veterans' families, and the general community they serve. Their focus remains on providing support for recreational activities, such as baseball, leadership programs for youth, and charitable and volunteer initiatives, specifically for the benefit of the veterans who have sacrificed for our great country. Additionally, money scholarships are provided to many deserving youth—the money generated from various fundraising activities such as food sales—including their fabulously successful, and popular Friday night fish frys. For the Ely Fagan Legion Post, it has always been about giving back to the Henrietta and neighboring Rochester-area communities, by providing wholesome, fun, recreational activities, and a much-needed helping hand to veterans in need.

On behalf of all the players from our 1967 Ely Fagan state championship baseball team, thank you Ely Fagan Post #1151 for the opportunities you gave us to play baseball, and for giving us the chance to represent you, your great work, and the American Legion programs of both the Rochester area and New York State. We are eternally thankful.

DEDICATION AND
SPECIAL ACKNOWLEDGMENTS

First, I recognize my lovely wife of 50 years, Judy, for her support, patience, and understanding, during the writing of this book, and for being my number one fan when I played baseball at Ithaca College. To my artist son Richard Jr., "thanks" for creating and providing this book's terrific cover art and illustration. Thanks also to my parents, grandparents, brother, and sister, who stood by me from Little League through College Baseball. They sacrificed by often putting their lives on the back burner in order to help get me to and from practices and games, and they were usually on the sidelines or in the stands watching and supporting me and our teams. They were amazing!

Second, I give thanks to all my coaches. Thanks to my first coaches, and also the best coaches a very young baseball player could ever hope for and have, Don Leege and Milt Leege. Thanks to my high school coaches Jack Stivers and Dan Topolski. Special thanks to my Ely Fagan Legion coach, Harold Petersen, who provided extraordinary support, inspiration, energy, and commitment to excellence. Without Mr. Petersen, the Ely Fagan team would not have come together and ultimately won the 1967 American Legion New York State Championship. Thanks to my Semi-Pro and Muni-League coach Jim Griffin. He, too, was a dedicated, and energetic coach who showed he cared about his players, and he always projected a positive, winning attitude. I thank my college coaches Hugh Hurst and the legendary Carlton

"Carp" Wood, for treating me and their other players like professionals. With Coach Wood there wasn't much fanfare and pomp, it was always about the team. He was a no-nonsense, businesslike baseball coach, a man of few words, who let his players play, and who had a special, low-key way of connecting with and getting the most from his pitchers and hitters.

Lastly, I thank all my terrific teammates for making my baseball experiences so meaningful, memorable, and fun. Foremost, special thanks go to my 1967 Ely Fagan teammates. This book is a tribute to you. Richie Petersen, Ralph Clapp, Al Pannoni, Rene Piccarreto, Don Leege, Billy Kreger, Joe Haefner, Andy Haefner, Chuck Glaza, John Kokinda, Gary Junge, and the late Bobby Porta and Joey Baldassare, I thank you all for providing those life-lasting baseball experiences. And, special thanks to Gary Junge, Al Pannoni, Rene Piccarreto, Don Leege, and Ralph Clapp for providing your baseball-life stories and contributions to this book. To my many talented, former-Ithaca College baseball teammates, thank you for sharing your college baseball experiences with me.

In closing, I leave you with one final, familiar baseball thought and exclamation.

"Let's Play Ball!"

ABOUT THE AUTHOR

Rich Goodwin, Sr. is a lifelong runner, having completed numerous races from 5K to full marathon distances over the past 45 years. He is a Vietnam-era army veteran, retired high school teacher, retired banker and insurance executive, former businessman, financial planner, and university assistant professor and adjunct professor of business, management, and economics.

Rich played 4 years of varsity baseball in high school, and Division I and II baseball at Ithaca College, where he received a BA in economics. He subsequently earned an MBA from the University of Connecticut.

Rich is also the author of the 2019 book, *Running Life Matters*, which celebrates the sport of running, the community of new and lifelong runners, and some of the valuable life lessons, experiences, and insights running provides.

Running Life Matters is available at Amazon, Barnes & Noble, and Shop.Booklogix.com, and it makes a great, entertaining, and inspirational gift for runners, former runners, and nonrunners alike!

Running Life Matters

By Richard Goodwin, Sr.

When all is said and done, I guess it's fair to say there are probably as many different running styles as there are runners. Truly, no two runners and running styles are identical! Running is a physical form of expression and universally, runners love to express themselves however, wherever and whenever they run. Running means different things to different people but at its essence, I think running's attraction is how it satisfies something in our primitive and core nature. It's the runner and the road, and all that's needed are some basic running clothes and running shoes (or not!) along with the motivation to make it happen. Once movement forward is unleashed, the rest takes care of itself—including affirmation of effort, insight, satisfaction, and the good health that results. After additional time and repetition, running can become a natural and vital life component.

Like relationships or friendships we make, I think we similarly establish a relationship with the running process and running itself when we decide to run. That initial commitment and relationship can be basic or superficial at first because we're just starting out and scratching the surface about what running is and what it means to run and be a runner. But over time we discover more about how running fits us and our lives, and how meaningful that running relationship becomes hinges somewhat on how we get along—how compatible we become. Running can, in some cases, truly become a partner, and for some, a lifelong partner as a result of many years devoted to running. The more of ourselves we give to running, the more running will give us in return. And like human relationships, the relationship we make with running can be full of ups and downs, doubt, insecurity, love, energy and fatigue, fulfillment, hope, promise, euphoria, disappointment, despair, pain—even suffering—and at times we can sometimes feel downright demoralized or even defeated. All in all, I've come to realize running is truly our friend and ally and that over time we learn to accept the ups, downs, and unpredictability connected with running. I don't believe we control running or that running controls us, nor do I think that should ever become a goal or objective. I think it's more a shared or symbiotic relationship with a mutually beneficial foundation built on give and take, mutual respect, understanding, tolerance, truth and trust. And isn't that, after all, the most promising and potentially healthiest and long-lasting relationship of all?

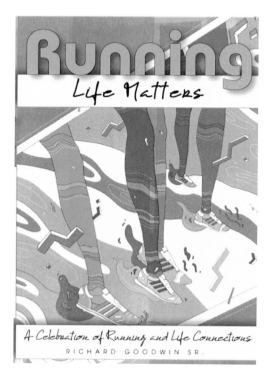